RANDOM SHOTS

FROM A

RIFLEMAN

Random Shots

from a

Rifleman

by

Captain John Kincaid

The Spellmount Library of Military History

SPELLMOUNT
Staplehurst

British Library Cataloguing in Publication Data:
A catalogue record for this book is available
from the British Library

Copyright © Spellmount Ltd 1998
Introduction © Ian Fletcher 1998

ISBN 1-86227-02-6

First published in 1835

This edition first published in the UK in 1998
in
The Spellmount Library of Military History
by
Spellmount Limited
The Old Rectory
Staplehurst
Kent TN12 0AZ

1 3 5 7 9 8 6 4 2

Printed in Great Britain by
T.J.International Ltd
Padstow, Cornwall

AN INTRODUCTION
By Ian Fletcher

When John Kincaid wrote his famous *Adventures in the Rifle Brigade*, publication attracted one of the kindest criticisms a book could receive, namely, that it was too short. This was the view expressed in the 'Monthly Magazine', and after receiving similarly good reviews, Kincaid was moved to put pen to paper once again and produce a second volume. Readers will see for themselves the sort of reception *Adventures* was accorded as extracts from some contemporary reviews can be found in this volume. The end result of Kincaid's further labours was *Random Shots from a Rifleman*, the 1835 first edition of which is faithfully reproduced here.

In this second volume Kincaid changes tack slightly, for *Random Shots* is much more anecdotal than *Adventures*, which chronicled his progress with the British army from the Walcheren campaign of 1809 – on which he scarcely commented – to the Waterloo campaign of June 1815. One feels as though the many anecdotes which are found here in this volume perhaps interrupted the flow of the story in *Adventures* and so were omitted. Happily for us, the success of Kincaid's first effort ensured that these anecdotes were published in this, his second volume.

Born in Stirlingshire in 1787, John Kincaid served in the 95th Rifles, the famous regiment, clad in green – or whatever came to hand once the rigours of campaigning took their toll – that were one of the ancestor's of today's Royal Green Jackets. The 5/60th, later the King's Royal Rifle Corps, was the other. The 95th gained a reputation for firing the first and last shots in Wellington's campaigns and few would argue that the regiment can claim with some justification to being the most famous of the many infantry regiments that served in the Peninsula and at Waterloo.

The 95th Rifles formed part of the famous Light Division in the Peninsula, along with the 43rd and 52nd Light Infantry regiments, and the 1st and 3rd Caçadores, the great supporters of their British brethren who, like the 95th, were armed with the superb Baker rifle. Save for a period of leave at the beginning of 1811, the Light Division was commanded by Robert Craufurd, the fiery Scot whose temper earned him the nickname 'Black Bob'. Craufurd was never loved by his men – neither overly was Wellington for that matter – but they respected him and knew his merits. Kincaid was one who knew that, after Craufurd was mortally wounded at the storming of Ciudad Rodrigo in January 1812, the division would never be the same again, and he was right. Under Craufurd, the Light Division blazed a trail up and down Portugal and Spain, getting into scrapes and skirmishes, achieving great feats, and courting controversy. When Craufurd died the division was placed under the command of Charles Alten, a steady and reliable soldier, but he was not Craufurd. Cynics may cry 'thank God for that', but without 'Black Bob', the Light Division was a shadow of its glorious best that had shone to advantage during the campaigns of 1810 and 1811.

The 95th, and indeed, the Light Division, achieved some great feats after Craufurd had departed. The Rifles still led from the front and were, as Kincaid wrote, the first in and last out of any action. Towards the end of the Peninsular War the 95th found itself in its element, amongst the hills and mountains of the Pyrenees, and in the lush, green, rolling landscape of southern France, which must have reminded them of home.

Their mode of fighting lent itself perfectly to the nature of the operations towards the end of 1813 when Wellington's army finally set foot on the sacred territory of France. And when Napoleon, forced to abdicate in April 1814, made his last bid for glory in March 1815 the 95th were there again, at Quatre Bras and at Waterloo where, on 18th June 1815, they witnessed the final showdown between the two great commanders of the age, Wellington and Napoleon. This, of course, is to show no disrespect to Marshal Blucher, whose Prussians arrived during the afternoon at Waterloo to swing the tide of victory in the Allies' favour, but it was the great clash of arms between 'Boney' and 'Old Nosey', the only time they ever met on the field of battle, which has so captured the imagination of the British public ever since. Kincaid served unscathed through all of this and was fortunate to be wounded only once during his entire service, at Foz d'Arouce in March 1811, during Massena's retreat from Portugal. How fortunate we are that he survived the blow and lived to tell us his tale.

When *Random Shots from a Rifleman* was published in 1835, it joined a growing library of similar books written by Wellington's veterans. And why not, for was it not natural that those who had taken part in the Great War, as it was known until 1914, would wish to place on record their own adventures and the part played by them in the downfall of the great ogre of the day, Napoleon Bonaparte? Literacy was on the increase and dozens were keen to tell their stories. After all, the Peninsular War was one of the most successful campaigns ever fought by a British army, and still is, and with the great campaign of 1815 coming so soon afterwards there was much to tell. Memoirs and letters began to be published as early as 1809 by the survivors of the Corunna campaign of 1808-09, followed by a steady stream of memoirs that appeared while the war was in progress.

Kincaid's *Adventures in the Rifle Brigade* appeared in 1830, two years after the first volume of William Napier's *History of the War in the Peninsula*, a great work which inspired dozens of veterans to put pen to paper. Unfortunately, more than a few of them turned to Napier when their own memories failed them. Thus, we must often beware of citing apparent eye-witnesses whose recollections are, however, drawn from reading Napier. Kincaid himself was not averse to drawing on Napier, particularly when he himself was not present. We also find him quoting Charles Cadell, of the 28th, whose own recollections were published in 1835, the same year as Kincaid's second book.

Random Shots begins with some tales obviously culled from the Officers' Mess of the 95th at Hythe, for they chiefly concern themselves with Sir John Moore's Corunna campaign, which concluded before Kincaid joined the regiment. But from then on we are treated to chapter after chapter of humorous and entertaining tales of life in Wellington's army and of the other side of glory. Kincaid was especially quick to pick up on any accidents that occurred either in camp, on the march, or even in battle. One can sympathise with Kincaid's comrades for his very keen eye must have hovered about them as a vulture hovers over its prey, waiting for some unfortunate mishap to befall the luckless.

The popularity of Kincaid's writings stems from a number of factors, not least his powers of description. It is hard not to let oneself be spirited away to the early 19th century when reading some passages of *Random Shots*, particularly those where he writes about life beneath the stars. And beneath the stars it often was, for tents did not become standard army issue until 1813. Kincaid and his fellow officers frequently slept wrapped in their cloaks, with a rock as their pillow and the night sky as their canopy. It was indeed a gypsy life which Wellington's men led, for of the 365 days in each year there may be just one or two major battles or sieges, leaving the bulk of the year to be spent in marching, in camp and on piquet duty.

Amongst the humour of *Random Shots* we find many pertinent observations and comments by Kincaid as to the relative merits and defects of equipment, of certain commanders, the Portuguese troops and the French, in fact, the whole spectrum of military affairs in Wellington's army. Much has been made of the qualities of Wellington's aristocratic officers, particularly those in the Foot Guards, and of their abilities to command. Kincaid himself regretted the fact that more aristocratic families did not send their sons into the army as they seemed to be able to command more willing obedience from their men with less effort than others. 'They were not better officers', he wrote, 'nor were they better or braver men than the soldiers of fortune, with which they were mingled; but there was a degree of refinement in all their actions, even in mischief, which commanded the respect of the soldiers, while those who had been framed in tougher moulds, and left unpolished, were sometimes obliged to have recourse to harsh measures to enforce it.' British army swords come in for their fair share of criticism when, in an oft-quoted passage, he wrote that the small regulation half-moon sabre 'was better calculated to shave a lady's maid than a Frenchman'.

Like many a British infantry officer, Kincaid had mixed views on the capabilities of the British cavalry. However, he was not alone in having nothing but praise for the cavalry of the King's German Legion, with whom the Light Division served with distinction during the operations on the Coa and Agueda rivers in the spring and summer of 1810. 'The first regiment of hussars,' he wrote, 'were associated with our division throughout the war, and were deserved favourites. In starting from a swampy couch and bowling along the road long ere dawn of day, it was one of the romances of a soldier's life to hear them chanting their national war songs – some three or four voices leading and the whole squadron joining in the chorus. As I have already said, they were no less daring in the field than they were surpassingly good on outpost duty. The hussar was at all times identified with his horse, he shared his bed and his board, and their movements were always regulated by the importance of their mission. If we saw a British dragoon at any time approaching in full speed, it excited no great curiosity among us, but whenever we saw one of the first hussars coming on at a gallop it was high time to gird on our swords and bundle up.' Kincaid was also fortunate to see at close quarters some of the famous men of the day such as Wellington, Craufurd, Beckwith and Barnard. He also had the privilege of serving with Julian Sanchez, the famous Spanish guerrilla leader, whose lancers were converted to regular cavalry at the end of the war, and is called 'the most celebrated throat-cutter in this part of the world.' It is interesting also, to note Kincaid expressing the thoughts of many a Peninsular veteran who bemoaned the fact that no medals had at the time been awarded for the campaign. Waterloo veterans were awarded a medal in 1816, the year after the great battle, but when Kincaid wrote *Random Shots* he did not know that the Peninsular army would have to wait until 1848 for the General Service Medal to be awarded, and you had to be alive, of course, to claim it. Kincaid himself received nine clasps – no mean achievement – for Fuentes de Oñoro, Ciudad Rodrigo, Badajoz, Salamanca, Vittoria, Pyrenees, Nivelle, Nive and Toulouse, in addition to his Waterloo medal, where he served as Adjutant to the 1st Battalion of the 95th.

John Kincaid served in the 95th Rifles for a further sixteen years after Waterloo and was promoted captain in 1826. He was knighted in 1852. It is ironic that, for a man whose adventures frequently brought him into contact with the beautiful, dark skinned ladies of Portugal and Spain, and whose amorous aspects of his life during the Peninsular War are very prominent throughout *Random Shots*, Kincaid never married. He came very close, however, when he saved a pair of sisters from the baying British mob during the terrible aftermath of the storming of Badajoz in April 1812. Kincaid fell in love with the younger sister but was not quick enough to prevent the inimitable Harry Smith, a fellow officer in the 95th, from stealing her away and marrying her. She followed her husband faithfully for the rest of his life and was immortalised by having the town of Ladysmith named after her. It could, however, have been so different had Kincaid been quicker off the mark. But such is fate.

The beauty of *Random Shots* is that, although it follows his campaigns between 1809 and 1815, its anecdotal style allows us to open its pages anywhere and find a source of great entertainment and amusement. There is a wealth of historical fact and detail but above all, this book is a most enjoyable and vivid account of campaign life in Wellington's army. The book will strike a chord with anybody who has travelled to the old campaign areas of Portugal and Spain, for they will recognise from Kincaid's descriptions the countryside that he himself is seeing, and with a bit of imagination they will, hopefully, sit back and see before them a picture of his gypsy lifestyle, the camp fires, the sound of brewing kettles, the echoing of bill hooks upon bark and the laughter and banter of the officers of the Light Division. John Kincaid would, no doubt, be delighted that, over 160 years on, his *Random Shots* were still finding their mark. So, go ahead and enjoy them.

Ian Fletcher
Rochester, 1998

TO

MAJOR-GENERAL

LORD FITZROY SOMERSET, K.C.B.

&c. &c. &c.

THIS VOLUME IS RESPECTFULLY INSCRIBED

BY HIS VERY OBEDIENT

AND VERY OBLIGED HUMBLE SERVANT,

J. KINCAID.

RANDOM SHOTS

FROM A

RIFLEMAN.

BY J. KINCAID,

Late Captain in, and Author of " Adventures in the Rifle Brigade."

LONDON:

T. AND W. BOONE, 29, NEW BOND-STREET.

M DCCC XXXV.

ADVENTURES IN THE RIFLE BRIGADE

IN THE

PENINSULA, FRANCE,

AND THE

NETHERLANDS,

From the Year 1809 to 1815;

By CAPTAIN JOHN KINCAID, First Battalion.

One vol. post 8vo. price 10s. 6d. boards.

" To those who are unacquainted with John Kincaid of the Rifles,—and few, we trow, of the old Peninsula bands are in this ignorant predicament, and to those who know him, we equally recommend the perusal of his book : it is a fac simile of the man,—a perfect reflection of his image, *veluti in speculo*. A capital Soldier, a pithy and graphic narrator, and a fellow of infinite jest. Captain Kincaid has given us, in this modest volume, the impress of his qualities, the *beau ideal* of a thorough-going Soldier of Service, and the faithful and witty history of some six years' honest and triumphant fighting.

" There is nothing extant in a Soldier's Journal, which, with so little pretension, paints with such truth and raciness the " domestic economy " of campaigning, and the downright business of handling the enemy.

" But we cannot follow further ;—recommending every one of our readers to pursue the Author himself to his crowning scene of Waterloo, where they will find him as quaint and original as at his *debut*. We assure them, it is not possible, by isolated extracts, to give a suitable impression of the spirit and originality which never flag from beginning to end of, Captain Kincaid's volume ; in every page of which he throws out flashes of native humour, a tithe of which would make the fortune of a Grub-street Bookmaker."—*United Service Journal.*

" We do not recollect one, among the scores of personal narratives, where the reader will find more of the realities of a Soldier's Life, or of the horrors that mark it; all is told gaily. but not unfeelingly."—*New Monthly Magazine, July.*

" His book has one fault, the rarest fault in books, it is too short."—*Monthly Magazine, April.*

" His book is one of the most lively histories of Soldiers' Adventures which have yet appeared; their entire freedom from affectation will sufficiently recommend them to a numerous class of readers."—*Athenæum.*

" *Kincaid's Adventures in the Rifle Brigade* is written with all the frankness and freedom from study which bespeaks the gallant soldier, one to whom the sword is more adapted than the pen, but who, as now *cedunt arma togæ*, has, in these ' piping times' of peace, determined to ' fight all his battles over again,' and he fights them in a style interesting and graphic. The remarks on the decisive termination of the Battle of Waterloo are striking and convincing; and to them and the whole book we refer our readers for much amusement and information."—*The Age.*

"This is an excellent and amusing book; and although it neither gives, nor pretends to give, lessons in strategy, or a true history of the great operations of our armies, we hold it to be a very instructive work. Napier, it is true, continues to be our textbook in the art of war; but, even in his work, there is something awanting, something which a due attention to historical etiquette prevents his conveying to us. He shows most satisfactorily the talents of our generals, and the *morale* of our army; but there is an insight into its composition which he cannot give us, and which, indeed, nothing can give but a wide personal acquaintance with military men, and lots of volumes like the present."—*Edinburgh Literary Journal.*

" Il est rare que les aventures arrivées à un seul personnage et racontées par lui intéressent le public au point de faire obtenir à ses mémoires un véritable succès; mais il en est autrement quand l'auteur a su habilement accompagner son histoire du récit de faits et d'événemens qui ont déjà fixé l'attention publique. L'ouvrage du Capitaine Kincaid est intéressant sous ces deux points de vue et sera favorablement accueilli. En même tems qu'on suit avec plaisir la marche de ses aventures, on recueille une foule de détails ignorés sur les campagnes de 1809 à 1815."—*Furet de Londres.*

NOTICE.

WHEN I sent my volume of " Adventures in the Rifle Brigade" into the world, some one of its many kind and indulgent critics was imprudent enough to say that " it had one fault, the rarest fault in books— it was too short ;" and while I have therefore endeavoured to acquit myself of such an unlooked-for charge by sending this additional one, I need only observe that if it also fails to satisfy, they may have " yet another."

Like its predecessor, this volume is drawn solely from memory, and of course open to error ; but of this my readers may feel assured, that it is free from romance; for even in the few soldiers' *yarns* which I have thought fit to introduce, the leading features are facts.

Lastly, in making my second editorial bow to the public, let me assure them that it is with no greater literary pretensions. I sent forth my first volume contrary to my own judgement; but rough and unpolished as it was, it pleased a numerous class of readers, and I therefore trust to be forgiven for marching past again to the same tune, in the hope that my *reviewing generals* may make the same favourable report of me in their orderly books.

ERRATUM.

Page 11, line 2, *for* remarkable, *read* remarkably.

CONTENTS.

CHAPTER I.

CHAP. II.

CHAP. III.

CHAP. IV.

CHAP. V.

CHAP. VI.

CHAP. VII.

CHAP. VII.

CHAP. VIII.

CHAP. IX.

CHAP. X.

CHAP. XI.

CHAP. XII.

CHAP. XIII.

RANDOM SHOTS

FROM

A RIFLEMAN.

CHAPTER I.

Family Pictures, with select Views of the Estate, fenced with distant Prospects.

EVERY book has a beginning, and the beginning of every book is the undoubted spot on which the historian is bound to parade his hero. The novelist may therefore continue to envelope his man in a fog as long as he likes, but for myself I shall at once unfold to the world that I am my own hero; and though that same world hold my countrymen to be rich in wants, with the article of modesty among them, yet do I hope to main-

tain the character I have assumed, with as much
propriety as can reasonably be expected of one
labouring under such a national infirmity, for

" I am a native of that land, which
    Some poets' lips and painters' hands"

have pictured barren and treeless.   But to shew
that these are mere fancy sketches, I need only
mention that as long as I remember anything,
there grew a bonny brier and sundry gooseberry
bushes in our kail-yard, and it was surrounded by
a stately row of pines, rearing their long spinster
waists and umbrella heads over the cabbages, as
carefully as a hen does her wings over her
brood of chickens, so that neither the sun nor
moon, and but a very few favoured stars had
the slightest chance of getting a peep therein,
nor had anything therein a chance of getting a
peep out, unless in the cabbages returning the
sheep's eyes of their star-gazers; for, while the
front was protected by a long range of house
and offices, with no ingress or egress but through
the hall-door, the same duty was performed on

the other three sides by a thick quick-set hedge which was impervious to all but the sparrows, so that the wondrous wise man of Islington might there have scratched his eyes out and in again a dozen times without being much the wiser.

My father was the laird and farmed the small property I speak of, in the lowlands of Stirlingshire, but he was unfortunately cut off in early life, and long before his young family were capable of appreciating the extent of their loss, and I may add, to the universal regret of the community to which he belonged; and in no country have I met, in the same walks of life, a body of men to equal in intelligence, prudence, and respectability, the small lowland Scotch laird.

Marrying and dying are ceremonies which almost every one has to go through at some period of his life, and from being so common, one would expect that they might cease to be uncommon; but people, nevertheless, still continue to look upon them as important events in

their individual histories. And while, with the
class I speak of, the joys of the one and the
grief at the other was as sensibly and unaffectedly
shewn as amongst any, yet with them the loss
of the head of the house produces no very
material change in the family arrangements; for
while in some places the proprietary of a sheep
confers a sort of patent of gentility upon the
whole flock, leaving as a bequest a scramble
for supremacy, yet the lowland laird is another
manner of man; one in fact who is not afraid
to reckon his chickens before they are hatched,
and who suffers no son of his to be born out of
his proper place. The eldest therefore steps
into his father's shoes as naturally as his father
steps out of them. The second is destined to
be a gentleman, that is, he receives a superior
education, and as soon as he is deemed qualified, he is started off with a tolerable outfit and
some ha'pence in his pocket to fulfil his destiny
in one of the armed or learned professions, while
the junior members of the family are put in such
other way of shifting for themselves as taste

and prudence may point out. And having thus, gentle reader, expounded as much of my family history as it behoveth thee to know, it only remains for me, with all becoming modesty, to introduce myself to you as, by birthright, the gentleman of the family, and without further ceremony to take you by the hand and conduct you along the path which I found chalked out for myself.

In my native country, as elsewhere, Dame Fortune is to be seen cutting her usual capers, and often sends a man starving for a life-time as a parson looking for a pulpit, a doctor dining on his own pills, or as a lawyer who has nothing to insert in his last earthly testament, who would otherwise have flourished on the top of a hay-stack, or as a cooper round a tar-barrel. How far she was indulgent in my case is a matter of moonshine. Suffice it that I commenced the usual process at the usual place, the parish school, under that most active of all teachers— Whipping,

> " That's Virtue's governess,
> Tutress of arts and sciences;
> That mends the gross mistakes of nature,
> And puts new life into dull matter."

And from the first letter in the alphabet I was successively flogged up through a tolerable quantity of English, some ten or a dozen books of Latin, into three or four of French, and there is no saying whether the cat-o'-nine tails, wielded by such a masterly hand, might not eventually have stirred me up as high as the woolsack, had not one of those tides in the affairs of school-boys brought a Leith merchant to a worthy old uncle of mine (who was one of my guardians) in search of a quill-driver, and turned the current of my thoughts into another channel. To be or not to be, that was the question; whether 'twere better to abide more stings and scourges from the outrageous cat, or to take the offer which was made, and end them.

It may readily be believed that I felt a suitable horror at the sight of the leathern instrument which had been so long and so ably administered for my edification, nor had I much greater affection for the learned professions as they loomed in perspective, for I feared the minister, hated the doctor, and had no respect for the lawyer, and in short it required but little persuasion to induce me to bind my prospects for the ensuing three years to the desk of a counting-house. I therefore took leave of my indefatigable preceptor, not forgetting to insert on the tablets of my memory, a promissory note to repay him stripe for stripe with legal interest, as soon as I should find myself qualified to perform the operation; but I need not add that the note (as all such notes usually are) was duly dishonoured; for, when I became capable of appreciating his virtues, I found him a worthy excellent man, and one who meant for the best; but I have lived to see that the schoolmaster of that day was all abroad.

The reminiscences of my three years' mercantile life leave me nothing worth recording, except that it was then I first caught a glimpse of my natal star.

I had left school as a school-boy, unconscious of a feeling beyond the passing moment. But the period at length arrived when Buonaparte's threatened invasion fired every loyal pair of shoulders with a scarlet coat. Mine were yet too slender to fill up a gap in the ranks, and my arm too weak to wield any thing more formidable than a drum-stick, but in devotion to the cause I would not have yielded to Don Quixote himself. The pride, pomp, and circumstance of glorious war had in fact set my soul in an unquenchable blaze, and I could think of nothing else. In reckoning up a column of pounds, shillings, and pence, I counted them but as so many soldiers, the rumbling of empty puncheons in the wine cellar sounded in my ears as the thunder of artillery, and the croaking voice of a weasand old watchman at " half-past twelve o'clock," as the hoarse challenge of the sentry from the ramparts.

My prospect of succeeding to the object on

which I had placed my affections were at the
time but slender, but having somewhere read
that if one did but set his eye on any thing
in reason, and pursued it steadily, he would
finally attain it, I resolved to adhere to such an
animating maxim, and fixing my heart on a
captain's commission, I pursued it steadily, and
for the encouragement of youth in all times to
come, I am proud to record that I finally did
attain it.

I returned to the country on the expiration of
my apprenticeship, which (considering the object
I had in view) happened at a most auspicious
moment; for the ensign of our parochial company of local militia had just received a commission in the line, and I was fortunate enough
to step into his vacated commission as well as
into his clothing and appointments.

I had by that time grown into a tall ramrod
of a fellow, as fat as a whipping-post—my predecessor had been a head and shoulders shorter,
so that in marching into his trousers I was
obliged to put my legs so far through them that

it required the eye of a *connoisseur* to distinguish whether they were not intended as a pair of breeches. The other end of my arms, too, were exposed to equal animadversion, protruding through the coat-sleeves to an extent which would have required a pair of gauntlets of the horse-guards blue to fill up the vacancy. Nevertheless, no peacock ever strutted more proudly in his plumage than I did in mine—and when I found myself on a Sunday in the front seat of the gallery of our parish church, exposed to the admiration of a congregation of milk-maids, my delight was without alloy.

CHAP. II.

" No man can tether time or tide,
The hour approaches Tam maun ride."
And he takes one side step and two front ones on the road
to glory.

It was a very fine thing, no doubt, to be an
ensign in the local militia, and a remarkable
pretty thing to be the admiration of all the
milk-maids of a parish, but while time was
jogging, I found myself standing with nothing
but the precarious footing of those pleasures to
stand upon, and it therefore behoved me to
think of sinking the ornamental for the sake of
the useful; and a neighbouring worthy, who
was an importer and vender of foreign timber,
happening at this time to make a proposition to

unite our fortunes, and that I should take the
charge of a branch establishment in the city of
Glasgow, it was arranged accordingly, and my
next position therefore was behind my own
desk in that Wapping of Glasgow, called the
Gorbals.

Mars, however, was still in the ascendant,
for my first transaction in the way of business
was to get myself appointed to a lieutenancy in
one of the volunteer regiments, and, as far as
I remember, I think that all my other transac-
tions while I remained there redounded more to
my credit as a soldier than as a citizen, and
when, at the end of the year, the offer of an
ensigncy in the militia enabled me to ascend a
step higher on the ladder of my ambition,
leaving my partner to sell or burn his sticks
(whichever he might find the most profitable), I
cut mine, and joined that finest of all militia
regiments, the North York, when I began to
hold up my head and to fancy myself something
like a soldier in reality.

Our movements during the short period that

I remained with them, were confined to casual changes among the different stations on the coasts of Kent and Sussex, where I got gradually initiated into all the mysteries of home service,—learnt to make love to the smugglers' very pretty daughters, and became a dead hand at wrenching the knocker from a door.

The idleness and the mischievous propensities of the officers of that district (of the line as well as the militia) were proverbial at the period I speak of; but, while as usual the report greatly exceeded the reality, there was this to be said in their behalf, that they were almost entirely excluded from respectable society; owing partly, perhaps, to their not being quite so select as at the present time, (those heroes who had a choice of pleasures preferring Almack's to Napoleon's balls,) but chiefly to the numbers of the troops with which those districts were inundated during the war, and which put it out of the power of individual residents to notice such a succession of military interlopers, unless they happened to be especially recommended to

them ; so that, as the Irishman expresses it—
he was a lucky cove indeed who in those days
succeeded in getting his legs under a gentleman's mahogany.

It is not therefore much to be wondered at,
if a parcel of wild young fellows thrown on
their own resources, when that warlike age required a larking spirit to be encouraged rather
than repressed amongst them,—I say, it is not to
be wondered at if they did occasionally amuse
themselves with a class of persons which,
under other circumstances, they would have
avoided, and if the consequences were sometimes what they had better not have been—but
the accounts between the man and woman of
that day having been long since closed, it is
not for me to re-open them, yet I remember
that even that manner of life was not without
its charms.

The only variety in my year's militia life was
an encampment on the lines at Chatham, where
we did duty on board the hulks, in the Medway.
My post was for the greater period with a guard

on board the old Irresistible, which was laden with about eight hundred heavy Danes who had been found guilty of defending their property against their invaders, and I can answer for it that they were made as miserable as any body of men detected in such a heinous crime had a right to be, for of all diabolical constructions in the shape of prisons the hulks claim by right a pre-eminence. However, we were then acting under the broad acknowledged principle, that those who are not for, are against us, and upon that same principle, the worthy Danes with their ships were respectfully invited to repose themselves for a while within our hospitable harbours.

On the breaking up of our encampment at Chatham we marched to Deal, where one of the periodical volunteerings from the militia, (to fill up the ranks of the line,) took place, and I need not add that I greedily snatched at the opportunity it offered to place myself in the position for which I had so long sighed.

On those occasions any subaltern who could

persuade a given number of men to follow him, received a commission in whatever regiment of the line he wished, provided there was a vacancy for himself and followers. I therefore chose that which had long been the object of my secret adoration, as well for its dress as the nature of its services and its achievements, the old ninety-fifth, now the Rifle Brigade.—" Hurrah for the first in the field and the last out of it, the bloody fighting ninety-fifth," was the cry of my followers while beating up for more recruits—and as glory was their object, a fighting and a bloody corps the gallant fellows found it, for out of the many who followed Captain Strode and me to it, there were but two serjeants and myself, after the sixth campaign, alive to tell the tale.

I cannot part from the good old North York without a parting tribute to their remembrance, for as a militia regiment they were not to be surpassed.—Their officers *were officers* as well as gentlemen, and there were few among them who would not have filled the same rank in the line with credit to themselves and to the service, and several wanted but the opportunity to turn up trumps of the first order.

I no sooner found myself gazetted than I took a run up to London to get rid of my loose cash, which being very speedily accomplished, I joined the regiment at Hythe barracks.

They had just returned from sharing in the glories and disasters of Sir John Moore's retreat, and were busily employed in organizing again for active service. I have never seen a regiment of more gallant bearing than the first battalion there shewed itself, from their brilliant chief, (the late Sir Sidney Beckwith), downwards; they were all that a soldier could love to look on; and, splendid as was their appearance, it was the least admirable part about them, for the beauty of their system of discipline consisted in their doing every thing that was necessary, and nothing that was not, so that every man's duty was a pleasure to him, and the *esprit de corps* was unrivalled.

There was an abundance of Johny Newcome's, like myself, tumbling in hourly, for it

was then such a favourite corps with the militia men, that they received a thousand men
over their complement within the first three days
of the volunteering, (and before a stop could be
put to it,) which compelled the horse-guards to
give an additional battalion to the corps.

On my first arrival my whole soul was so
absorbed in the interest excited by the service-
officers that, for a time, I could attend to nothing else—I could have worshipped the different relics that adorned their barrack-rooms
—the pistol or the dagger of some gaunt
Spanish robber—a string of beads from the
Virgin Mary of some village chapel—or the
brazen helmet of some French dragoon, taken
from his head after it had parted company with
his shoulders, and with what a greedy ear did
I swallow the stories of their hair-breadth 'scapes
and imminent perils, and long for the time when
I should be able to make such relics and such
tales mine own. Fate has since been propitious,
and enabled me to spin as long a yarn as most
folks, but as some of their original stories still

dwell with much interest on my memory, I shall quote one or two of them, in the hope that they may not prove less so to my readers, for I am not aware that they have yet been published.

ANECDOTE THE FIRST.

Of all the vicissitudes of the late disastrous campaign, I found that nothing dwelt so interestingly on the remembrance of our officers as their affair at Calcabellos—partly because it was chiefly a regimental fight, and partly because they were taken at a disadvantage, and acquitted themselves becomingly.

The regiment was formed in front of Calcabellos covering the rear of the infantry, and on the first appearance of the enemy they had been ordered to withdraw behind the town. Three parts of them had already passed the bridge, and the remainder were upon it, or in the act of filing through the street with the careless confidence which might be expected from their knowledge that the British cavalry still stood between them and the enemy; but in an instant our own cavalry, without the slightest notice, galloped through and over them, and the same instant saw a French sabre flourishing over the head of every man who remained beyond the bridge—many were cut down in the streets, and a great portion of the rear company were taken prisoners.

The remainder of the regiment, seeing the unexpected attack, quickly drew off among the vineyards to the right and left of the road, where they coolly awaited the approaching assault. The dismounted voltigeurs first swarmed over the river, assailing the riflemen on all sides, but they were met by a galling fire, which effectually stopped them. General Colbert next advanced to dislodge them, and passing the river at the head of his dragoons, he charged furiously up the road; but, when within a few yards of our men, he was received with such a deadly fire, that scarcely a Frenchman remained in the saddle, and the general himself was among the

slain. The voltigeurs persevered in their unsuccessful endeavours to force the post, and a
furious fight continued to be waged, until
darkness put an end to it, both sides having
suffered severely.

Although the principal combat had ceased
with the day-light, the riflemen found that the
troubles and the fatigues of twenty-four hours
were yet in their infancy, for they had to
remain in the position until ten at night, to give
the rest of the army time to fall back, during
which they had to sustain several fierce assaults,
which the enemy made, with the view of ascertaining whether our army were on the move;
but in every attempt they were gallantly repulsed,
and remained in ignorance on the subject until
day-light next morning. Our people had, in
the meantime, been on the move the greater
part of the night, and those only who have done
a mile or two of vineyard walking in the dark,
can form an adequate notion of their twenty-
four hours work.

General Colbert (the enemy's hero of the

day) was, by all accounts, (if I may be permitted
the expression,) splendid as a man, and not less
so as a soldier. From the commencement of
the retreat of our army he had led the advance,
and been conspicuous for his daring: his gallant
bearing had, in fact, excited the admiration of
his enemies; but on this day, the last of his
brilliant earthly career, he was mounted on a
white charger, and had been a prominent figure
in the attack of our men in the street the instant
before, and it is not, therefore, to be wondered
at if the admiration for the soldier was for a
space drowned in the feeling for the fallen comrades which his bravery had consigned to death;
a rifleman, therefore, of the name of Plunket,
exclaiming, " thou too shalt surely die!" took
up an advanced position, for the purpose of
singling him out, and by his hand he no doubt
fell.

Plunket was not less daring in his humble
capacity than the great man he had just brought
to the dust. He was a bold, active, athletic
Irishman, and a deadly shot; but the curse of

his country was upon him, and I believe he was finally discharged, without receiving such a recompense as his merits in the field would otherwise have secured to him.

ANECDOTE THE SECOND.

In one of the actions in which our regiment was engaged, in covering the retreat to Corunna, a superior body of the enemy burst upon the post of a young officer of the name of Uniacke, compelling him to give way in disorder, and in the short scramble which followed, he very narrowly escaped being caught by the French officer who had led the advance,—a short stout fellow, with a cocked hat, and a pair of huge jack-boots.

Uniacke was one of the most active men in the army, and being speedily joined by his supporting body, which turned the tables upon his adversary, he resolved to give his *friend* a sweat in return for the one he had got, and started

after him, with little doubt, from his appearance
and equipment, that he would have him by the
neck before he had got many yards further;
but, to his no small mortification, the stout gentleman plied his seven-league boots so cleverly
that Uniacke was unable to gain an inch upon
him.

ANECDOTE THE THIRD.

At Astorga, a ludicrous alarm was occasioned
by the frolic of an officer; though it might have
led to more serious results.

The regiment was quartered in a convent, and
the officers and the friars were promiscuously
bundled for the night on mattresses laid in one
of the galleries; when, about midnight, Captain —— awaking, and seeing the back of one
of the Padres looking him full in the face, from
under the bed-clothes, as if inviting the slap of
a fist, he, acting on the impulse of the moment,
jumped up, and with a hand as broad as a coal-

shovel, and quite as hard, made it descend on the bottom of the astounded sleeper with the force of a paviour, and then stole back to his couch. The Padre roared a hundred murders, and murder was roared by a hundred Padres, while the other officers, starting up in astonishment, drew their swords and began grappling with whoever happened to be near them. The uproar, fortunately, brought some of the attendants with lights before any mischief happened, when the cause of the disturbance was traced, to the no small amusement of every one. The offender tried hard to convince the afflicted father that he had been under the influence of a dream; but the four fingers and the thumb remained too legibly written on the offended spot to permit him to swallow it.

ANECDOTE THE FOURTH.

When the straggling and the disorders of the army on the retreat to Corunna became so

C

serious as to demand an example, Sir Edward
Paget, who commanded the reserve, caused two
of the plunderers to be tried by a court-martial,
and they were sentenced to suffer death. The
troops were ordered to parade in front of the
town, to witness the execution, but, while in
the act of assembling, a dragoon came galloping in from the front to inform Sir Edward
by desire of his brother (Lord Paget), that the
enemy were on the move, and that it was time
for the infantry to retire. Sir Edward, however,
took no notice of the message. The troops
assembled, and the square was formed, when a
second dragoon arrived, to say that the enemy
were advancing so rapidly that if Sir Edward
did not immediately retire, his lordship could
not be answerable for the consequences. Sir
Edward, with his usual coolness and determination, said he cared not, for he had a
duty to perform, and were the enemy firing into
the square, that he would persevere with it.
Dragoon after dragoon, in rapid succession,
galloped in with a repetition of the message :

still the preparations went on, and by the time they were completed, (and it wanted but the word of command to launch the culprits into eternity,) the clang of the carabines of the retreating dragoons was heard all around.

In the breast of Sir Edward, it is probable, that the door of mercy never had been closed, and that he had only waited until the last possible moment to make it the more impressive; and impressive truly it must have been; nor is it easy to imagine such a moment; for, independently of the solemn and desolate feeling with which one at all times witnesses the execution of a comrade, let his offence be what it may, they had an additional intensity on this occasion, on the score of their own safety; for, brief as the span seemed to be that was allotted to the culprits, the clang of the carabine, and the whistling ball, told that it was possible to be even still more brief on the parts of many of the spectators.

Sir Edward, however, now addressed the troops, with a degree of coolness which would argue that danger and he had been long

familiar. He pointed out the enormity of the
offence of which the culprits had been guilty,
that they deserved not to be saved, and that
though the enemy were now upon them, and
might lay half their number dead while witnessing the execution, that only one thing would
save them, and that was, " would the troops
now present pledge themselves that this should
be the last instance of insubordination that
would occur in the course of the retreat ?" A
simultaneous " Yes," burst from the lips of the
assembled thousands, and the next instant saw
the necessary measures taken to check the advancing foe, while the remainder resumed their
retreat, lightened of a load of care, which a few
minutes before had been almost intolerable.

The conduct of these regiments, as compared
with others, was very exemplary during the
retreat, although their duty, in protecting the
stragglers of the army till the last possible
moment, was of the most harassing kind.
They had no means of punishing those to whom
they were indebted for their extra trouble, but

by depriving them of their ill-gotten gains, so
that whenever a fellow came in with a bag of
flour under his arm, (which was no uncommon
occurrence,) they made it a rule to empty the
bag over his head, to make him a marked man.
Napier says of them, that " for twelve days
these hardy soldiers covered the retreat, during
which time they had traversed eighty miles of
road in two marches, passed several nights under
arms in the snow of the mountains, were seven
times engaged with the enemy, and now assembled at the outposts (before Corunna), having
fewer men missing from the ranks, including
those who had fallen in battle, than any other
division in the army."*

I shall now, with the reader's permission, resume the thread of my narrative.

---

* The foregoing story, I find, has just made its appearance
in a volume published by Lieutenant-Colonel Cadell; but as
this narrative was publicly noticed, as being in preparation,
prior to the publication of his, I have not thought it necessary
to expunge it.

CHAP. III.

An old one takes to his heels, leaving a young one in arms.—
The dessert does not always follow the last course of—a
goose.—Goes to the war, and ends in love.

In those days, the life of a soldier was a stirring
and an active one. I had not joined the regiment above a fortnight when the 1st battalion
received orders for immediate active service, and
General Graham was to make his appearance on
the morrow, to inspect them prior to their embarkation. Every man destined for service was
to appear in the ranks, and as my turn had not
yet come, I was ordered, the previous evening,
to commence my career as a rifleman, in charge
of the guard; and a most unhappy *debut* I made

of it, and one that argued but little in behalf of my chances of future fame in the profession.

My guard was composed of the Lord knows who, for, excepting on the back of the sergeant, I remember that there was not a rag of uniform amongst them. I was too anxious to forget all about them to think of informing myself afterwards; but, from what I have since seen, I am satisfied that they must either have been a recent importation from " the first gem of the sea," or they had been furnished for the occasion by the governor of Newgate;—however, be that as it may, I had some ten or a dozen prisoners handed over to me; and as my eye was not sufficiently practised to distinguish, in such a group, which was the soldier and which the prisoner, I very discreetly left the whole affair to the sergeant, who seemed to be a man of *nous.* But while I was dozing on the guard-bed, about midnight, I was startled by a scramble in the soldier's room, and the cry of " guard, turn out;" and, on running out to ascertain the cause, the sergeant told me that the light in the

guard-house had been purposely upset by some
one, and, suspecting that a trick was intended,
he had turned out the guard ; and truly his suspicions were well-grounded, although he took
an erroneous method of counteracting it; for,
the sentry over the door, not being a much
shrewder fellow than myself in distinguishing
characters in the dark, in suffering the guard to
turn out, had allowed some of the prisoners to
turn out too, and, amongst the rest, one who
had been reserved for an especial example of
some sort or other, and whose absence was
likely to make a noise in the neighbourhood.

This was certainly information enough to furnish me with food for reflection for the remainder
of the night, and, as if to enhance its *agreeable*
nature, the sergeant-major paid me a visit at
daylight in the morning, and informed me that
such things did sometimes happen;—he enume-
rated several cases of the kind in different regiments, and left me with the consolatory piece of
information that the officer of the guard had on
each occasion been *allowed* to retire without a

court-martial !!! My readers, I am sure, will rejoice with me that in this, as in other cases, there is no rule without an exception, for otherwise they would never have had the pleasure of reading a book of mine.

How I had the good fortune to be excepted on that occasion I never found out; probably, in the hurry and bustle of preparation it was overlooked, —or, probably, because they hoped better things of me thereafter,—but my commanding officer never noticed it, and his kindness in so doing put me more on the alert for the future than if he had written a volume of censure.

Among the other novelties of the aforesaid guard-house on that memorable night, I got acquainted with a very worthy goose, whose services in the Rifle Brigade well merit a chapter in its history. If any one imagines that a goose is a goose he is very much mistaken : and I am happy in having the power of undeceiving him, for I am about to show that my (or rather our regimental) goose was shrewd, active, and intelligent, it was a faithful public servant, a social

companion, and an attached friend, (I wish that
every biped could say but half so much). Its
death, or its manner of departure from this
world, is still clouded in mystery; but while
my book lives, the goose's memory shall not die.
It had attached itself to the guard-house
several years prior to my appearance there, and
all its doings had been as steady as a sentry-box:
its post was with the sentry over the guard; in
fine weather it accompanied him in his walk,
and in bad, it stood alongside of him in his box.
It marched with the officer of the guard in all
his visiting rounds, and it was the first on all
occasions to give notice of the approach of any
one in authority, keeping a particularly sharp
look-out for the captain and field-officer of the
day, whether by day or night. The guard might
sleep, the sentry might sleep, but the goose was
ever wide awake. It never considered itself
relieved from duty, except during the breakfast
and dinner-hours, when it invariably stepped
into the guard-house, and partook of the soldiers'
cheer, for they were so devotedly attached to it

that it was at all times bountifully supplied, and it was not a little amusing, on those occasions, to see how the fellow cackled whenever the soldiers laughed, as if it understood and enjoyed the joke as much as they did.

I did not see Moore's Almanack for 1812, and, therefore, know not whether he predicted that Michaelmas would be fatal to many of the tribe that year; but I never saw a comrade more universally lamented than the poor goose was when the news of its mysterious disappearance reached us in Spain.

Our comrades at home, as a last proof of their affection, very magnanimously offered a reward of ten pounds for the recovery of the body, dead or alive; but whether it filled a respectable position in a banquet of that year, or still lives to bother the decayed tooth of some elderly maiden, at Michaelmas next, remains to be solved.

On the 24th of March, 1809, our first battalion received orders to march at midnight for Dover, there to be united with the 43d and 52d regiments, as a light brigade, under Major-

General Robert Crawfurd, and to embark next morning to join the army which was then assembling in the Peninsula.

In marching for embarkation in those stirring times, the feeling of the troops partook more of the nature of a ship's crew about to sail on a roving commission, than a land-crab expedition which was likely to prove eternal; for although one did occasionally see some blubber-headed fellow mourning over his severed affections for a day or two, yet a thorough-going one just gave a kiss to his wife, if he had one, and two to his sweetheart, if he had not, and away he went with a song in his mouth.

I now joined the 2d battalion, where we were not permitted to rest long on our oars, for, within a month, we were called upon to join the expedition with which

" The Great Earl of Chatham, and a hundred thousand men,
    Sailed over to Holland, and then sailed back again."

As the military operations of that expedition

do not entitle them to a place in such an important history as mine is, I shall pass them over, simply remarking that some of our companies fired a few professional shots, and some of our people got professionally shot, while a great many more visited Death by the doctor's road, and almost all who visited him not, got uncommonly well shaken.

South Beeveland ultimately became our headquarters. It is a fine island, and very fertile, yielding about forty bushels of frogs an acre, and tadpoles enough to fence it with. We were there under the command of General W. Stewart, whose active mind, continually in search of improvement, led him to try (in imitation of some foreign customs) to saddle the backs of the officers with knapsacks, by way of adding to their comfort; for he proved to demonstration that if an officer had a clean shirt in his knapsack on his back, that he might have it to put on at the end of his day's march; whereas, if he had it not on his own back, it might be left too far back to be of use to him when wanted.

This was a fact not to be disputed, but so wedded were we to ancient prejudices that we remained convinced that the shirt actually in wear, with all its additions at the end of an extra day or two, must still weigh less than the knapsack with a shirt in it; and upon those grounds we made a successful kick, and threw them off, not, however, until an experimental field-day had been ordered to establish them. The order required that each officer should parade in a knapsack, or something answering the same purpose, and it was amusing enough to see the expedients resorted to, to evade, without committing a direct breach of it. I remember that my apology for one on that occasion was slinging an empty black oil-skin haversack knapsack-ways, which looked so much like a newly-lanced blister on my back that it made both the vraws and the frogs stare. The attempt was never repeated.

What a singular change did a short residence in that pestiferous place work in the appearance of our army! It was with our regiment as with others; one month saw us embark a thousand men at Deal, in the highest health and spirits, and the next month saw us land, at the same place, with about seven hundred men, carrying to hospital, or staggering under disease.

I cannot shake off that celebrated Walcheren fever without mentioning what may or may not be a peculiarity in it;—that a brother-officer and I experienced a return of it within a day of each other, after a lapse of five years, and again, within a week, after the lapse of the following three years.

As my heart had embarked for the Peninsula with the 1st battalion, although my body (for the reasons given) remained behind for a year, I shall, with the reader's permission, follow the first, as being in the more interesting position of the two; and although, under these circumstances, I am not permitted to speak in the first person singular until the two shall be again united, yet whatever I do speak of I have heard so often and so well authenticated, that I am enabled to give it with the same confidence as if I had been an eye-witness.

" A LAY OF LOVE FOR LADY BRIGHT."

Lisbon was doubtless as rich in abominations now as it was a year after, without any other redeeming virtue, which is a very ugly commencement to a tale of love; but having landed my reader a second time at the same place, I am anxious to relieve him from the fear of being treated to a second edition of the same story, and to assure him that my head-piece has been some time charged with fresh ammunition and I mean to discharge it now, to prevent its getting rusty. I intend to fight those battles only that I never fought before, galloping over the ground lightly, and merely halting to give a little of my conversation, such as it is, whenever I have anything new to tell; and as I have no idea of enduring the fatigues of the march to Talavera, nor the pleasures of fattening on the dinners of chopped straw which followed it, I shall leave my regiment to its fate until its return to the north of Portugal, and take advantage of the repose it affords to make my editorial bow with all due deference to my fair and lovely readers, to express my joy that I have been once more enabled to put myself in communion with them, and to assure them of my continued unbounded love and admiration, for I feel and have ever felt that the man who gave frailty the name of woman was a blockhead, and must have been smarting under some unsuccessful bit of the tender, for I have met her in the bower and in the battle, and have ever found her alike admirable in both! That old fool Shakspeare, too, having only a man's courage to meet a sprite with! Had he but told Macbeth to dare as woman dared, he would have seen the ghost of Banquo vanish into the witches' kettle in the twinkling of a wheelbarrow; for although I have never seen a woman kick the bucket, I have certainly seen her kick every thing else, and in fact there is nothing in the heroics that I have not seen her do. See her again when she descends into herself, and it is very odd if I have not seen

her there too! for no man has ever been so
often or so deep in love as I have—my poor
heart has been lacerated, torn, and finally
scorched until it is withered up like a roasted
potato with scarcely the size of a kiss left.

How it was that I did not find myself dangling
at a door-post by the end of a silk handkerchief
some odd morning is to me astonishing, but
here I am, living and loving still as fondly as
ever. Prudence at this moment whispers that
I have said enough for the present, for if I go
on making love so fiercely thus early in the day,
I shall be forced to marry the whole sex and
bring my book to a premature conclusion, for
which posterity would never forgive me. I must
therefore for the present take a most reluctant
leave, with a promise of renewing my courtship
from time to time as opportunities offer, if they
will but good-naturedly follow me through the
various scenes into which I am about to conduct
them; and while I do my best to amuse them
by the way, should I unintentionally dive so

deeply into the pathetic as to beguile them of a tear, let me recommend them to wipe it away, for it is only their smiles I court.

While on the way to join the light division on the northern frontier, I shall take the opportunity of introducing the reader to their celebrated commander, the late Major-General Robert Crawfurd, an officer who, for a length of time, was better known than liked, but like many a gem of purer ray his value was scarcely known until lost.

CHAP. IV.

Shewing how generals may descend upon particulars with
a cat-o'-nine tails. Some extra Tales added, Historical,
Comical, and Warlike all.

CRAWFURD was no common character. He,
like a gallant cotemporary of his, was not born
to be a great general, but he certainly was a distinguished one,—the history of his division and
the position which he held beyond the Coa in
1810, attest the fact. He had neither judgement, temper, nor discretion to fit him for a
chief, and as a subordinate he required to be
held with a tight rein, but his talents as a
general of division were nevertheless of the first
order. He received the three British regiments

under his command, finished by the hands of a
master in the art, Sir John Moore, and, as
regiments, they were faultless; but to Crawfurd
belonged the chief merit of making them the
war brigade which they became, alike the admiration of their friends and foes. How he
made them so I am about to show, but how
such another is to be made now that his system
has fallen into disrepute, will be for futurity to
determine.

I think I see a regiment of those writers
who are just now taking the cat by the tail,
parading for a day's march under that immortal
chief—that he furnishes them with an ink-bottle
for a canteen, fills their knapsacks with foolscap, their mouths with mouldy biscuit, and
starts them off with sloped pens. They go along
with the buoyancy of a corps of reporters reconnoitring for a memorandum, and they very
quickly catch one and a Tartar to the bargain,
for the monotony of the road is relieved by the
crossing of a fine broad stream, and over the
stream is a very fine plank to preserve the polish

of Warren's jet on the feet of the pedestrian—
they all jump gaily towards the plank, but they
are pulled up by a grim gentleman with a drawn
sword, who, with a voice of thunder, desires
them to keep their ranks and march through
the stream. Well! this is all mighty pleasant,
but now that they are up to their middles in
the water, there surely can be no harm in
stopping half a minute to lave a few handfuls
of it into their parched mouths. I think I
see the astonishment of their editorial nerves
when they find a dozen lashes well bestowed
a posteriori upon each, by way of their further
refreshment and clearing off scores for that
portion of the day's work (for the General
was a man who gave no credit on those occasions). He had borrowed a leaf from the
history of the land-crabs, and suffered neither
mire nor water to disturb the order of his march
with impunity.

Now I daresay he would have had to flog an
editor a dozen times before he had satisfied him
that it was to his advantage; but a soldier is

open to conviction, and such was the manner of
making one of the finest and most effective
divisions that that or any other army ever saw.

Where soldiers are to be ruled, there is
more logic in nine tails of a cat than in the
mouths of a hundred orators; it requires very
little argument to prove, and I'll defy the most
eloquent preacher, (with the unknown tongue
to boot,) to persuade a regiment to ford a river
where there is a bridge to conduct them over
dry-shod, or to prevent them drinking when
they are in that river if they happen to feel
thirsty, let him promise them what he will as a
reward for their obedience. It is like preaching
to his own flock on the subject of their eternal
welfare (and I make the comparison with all
due reverence); they would all gladly arrive at
the end he aims at, but at the same time how
few will take the necessary steps to do so, and
how many prefer their momentary present enjoyment? So it was with the soldiers, but with
this difference, that Crawfurd's cat forced them
to take the right road whether they would or

no, and the experiment once made carried conviction with it, that the comfort of every individual in the division materially depended on the rigid exaction of his orders, for he shewed that on every ordinary march he made it a rule to halt for a few minutes every third or fourth mile, (dependent on the vicinity of water,) that every soldier carried a canteen capable of containing two quarts, and that if he only took the trouble to fill it before starting, and again, if necessary, at every halt, it contained more than he would or ought to drink in the interim; and that therefore every pause he made in a river for the purpose of drinking was disorderly, because a man stopping to drink delayed the one behind him proportionately longer, and so on progressively to the rear of the column.

In like manner the filing past dirty or marshy parts of the road in place of marching boldly through them or filing over a plank or narrow bridge in place of taking the river with the full front of their column in march, he proved to demonstration on true mathematical principles, that with the numbers of those obstacles usually encountered on a day's march, it made a difference of several hours in their arrival at their bivouac for the night. That in indulging by the way, they were that much longer labouring under their load of arms, ammunition, and necessaries, besides bringing them to their bivouac in darkness and discomfort; it very likely, too, got them thoroughly drenched with rain, when the sole cause of their delay had been to avoid a partial wetting, which would have been long since dried while seated at ease around their camp-fires; and if this does not redeem Crawfurd and his cat, I give it up.

The general and his divisional code, as already hinted at, was at first much disliked; probably, he enforced it, in the first instance, with unnecessary severity, and it was long before those under him could rid themselves of that feeling of oppression which it had inculcated upon their minds. It is due, however, to the memory of the gallant general to say that punishment for those disorders was rarely necessary after the first campaign; for the system, once established, went on like clock-work, and the soldiers latterly became devotedly attached to him; for while he exacted from them the most rigid obedience, he was, on his own part, keenly alive to every thing they had a right to expect from him in return, and woe befel the commissary who failed to give a satisfactory reason for any deficiencies in his issues. It is stated that one of them went to the commander-in-chief to complain that he had been unable to procure bread for the light division, and that General Crawfurd had threatened that if they were not supplied within a given time, he would put him in the guard-house. " Did he ?" said his lordship; " then I would recommend you to find the bread, for if he said so, by ——, he'll do it !"

Having in this chapter flogged every man who had any shadow of claim to such a distinction, I shall now proceed and place myself along with my regiment to see that they prove themselves worthy of the *pains* taken in their instruction.

From the position which the light division then held, their commander must have been fully satisfied in his own mind that their military education had not been neglected, for *certes* it required every man to be furnished with a clear head, a bold heart, and a clean pair of heels— all three being liable to be put in requisition at any hour by day or night. It was no place for reefing topsails and making all snug, but one which required the crew to be constantly at quarters; for, unlike their nautical brethren, the nearer a soldier's shoulders are to the rocks the less liable he is to be wrecked—and there they had more than enough of play in occupying a front of twenty-five miles with that small division and some cavalry. The chief of the 1st German hussars meeting our commandant one morning, " Well, Colonel," says the gallant German in broken English, " how you do?" " O, tolerably well, thank you, considering that I am obliged to sleep with one eye open." " By Gott," says the other, " I never sleeps at all."

Colonel Beckwith at this time held the pass

of Barba del Puerco with four companies of the
Rifles, and very soon experienced the advantage
of having an eye alive, for he had some active
neighbours on the opposite side of the river who
had determined to beat up his quarters by way
of ascertaining the fact.

The *Padrè* of the village, it appeared, was a
sort of vicar of Bray, who gave information to
both sides so long as accounts remained pretty
equally balanced between them, but when the
advance of the French army for the subjugation
of Portugal became a matter of certainty, he
immediately chose that which seemed to be the
strongest, and it was not ours.

The *Padrè* was a famous hand over a glass
of grog, and where amusements were so scarce,
it was good fun for our youngsters to make
a *Padrè* glorious, which they took every
opportunity of doing; and as is not unusual
with persons in that state, (laymen as well as
Padrès,) he invariably fancied himself the only
sober man of the party, so that the report was
conscientiously given when he went over to the

French General Ferey, who commanded the division opposite, and staked his reputation as a *Padrè*, that the English officers in his village were in the habit of getting blind drunk every night, and that he had only to march over at midnight to secure them almost without resistance.

Ferey was a bold enterprising soldier, (I saw his body in death after the battle of Salamanca); he knew to a man the force of the English in the village, and probably did not look upon the attempt as very desperate were they even at their posts ready to receive him; but as the chances seemed to be in favour of every enemy's head being " nailed to his pillow," the opportunity was not to be resisted, and accordingly, at midnight on the 19th of March, he assembled his force silently at the end of the bridge. The shadows of the rocks which the rising moon had just cast over the place prevented their being seen, and the continuous roar of the mountain torrent, which divided them, prevented their being heard even by our double sentry posted at the other end of the bridge within a few yards of them. Leaving a powerful support to cover his retreat in the event of a reverse, Ferey at the head of six hundred chosen grenadiers burst forth so silently and suddenly, that, of our double sentry on the bridge, the one was taken and the other bayonetted without being able to fire off their pieces. A sergeant's party higher up among the rocks had just time to fire off as an alarm, and even the remainder of the company on picquet under O'Hare had barely time to jump up and snatch their rifles when the enemy were among them. O'Hare's men, however, though borne back and unable to stop them for an instant, behaved nobly, retiring in a continued hand-to-hand personal encounter with their foes to the top of the pass, when the remaining companies under Sidney Beckwith having just started from their sleep, rushed forward to their support, and with a thundering discharge, tumbled the attacking column into the ravine below, where, passing the bridge under cover of the

fire of their supporting body, they resumed
their former position, minus a considerable
number of their best and bravest. The colonel,
while urging the fight, observed a Frenchman
within a yard or two, taking deliberate aim
at his head. Stooping suddenly down and
picking up a stone, he immediately shyed it at
him, calling him at the same time a " scoundrel,
to get out of that." It so far distracted the
fellow's attention that while the gallant Beckwith's cap was blown to atoms, the head remained
untouched.

The whole concern was but the affair of a few
minutes, but we nevertheless looked upon it as
no inconsiderable addition to our regimental
feather, for the appointed alarm post of one of
the companies had carried it to a place where it
happened that they were not wanted, so that
there were but three companies actually engaged ; and therefore with something less than
half their numbers they had beaten off six
hundred of the *élite* of the French army. But
our chief pride arose from its being the first and

last night-attempt which the enemy ever made to surprise a British post in that army.

Of the worthy pastor I never heard more—I know not whether the bold Ferey paid the price of the information he had brought, in gold, or with an ounce of lead; but certain it is that his flock were without ghostly consolation during the remainder of our sojourn—not that it was much sought after at that particular time, for the village damsels had already begun running up a score of *peccadillos*, and it was of little use attempting to wipe it out until the final departure of their heretical visitors.

Among the wounded who were left on the field by the enemy, there was a French sergeant whom I have often heard our officers speak of with much admiration—he was a fine handsome young fellow, alike romantic in his bravery, and in devotion to his emperor and his country— he had come on with the determination to conquer or to die, and having failed in the first, he seemed resolved not to be balked in the other, which a ball through a bad part of the thigh had placed him in the high road for, and he, therefore, resisted every attempt to save him, with the utmost indignation, claiming it as a matter of right to be allowed to die on the field where he had fallen. Our good, honest, rough diamonds, however, who were employed in collecting the wounded, were equally determined that the point in dispute should only be settled between him and the doctor in the proper place, and accordingly they shouldered him off to the hospital whether he would or no. But even there he continued as untameable as a hyena— his limb was in such a state that nothing but amputation could save his life—yet nothing would induce him to consent to it—he had courage to endure any thing, but nothing could reconcile him to receive any thing but blows from his enemies. I forget how, or in what way, the amputation of the limb was at length accomplished. To the best of my recollection death had already laid a hand upon him, and it was done while he was in a state of insensibility. But be that as it may, it was done, and the danger and the fit of heroics having travelled with the departed limb, he lived to thank his preservers for the brotherly kindness he had experienced at their hands, and took a grateful and affectionate farewell of them when his health was sufficiently restored to permit his being removed to the care of his countrymen.

Shortly after this affair at Barba del Puerco the French army under Massena came down upon Ciudad Rodrigo, preparatory to the invasion of Portugal, and obliged the light division to take up a more concentrated position.

It is not my intention to take notice of the movements of the army further than is necessary to illustrate the anecdotes I relate; but I cannot, on this occasion, resist borrowing a leaf out of Napier's admirable work, to shew the remarkable state of discipline which those troops had been brought to—for while I have no small portion of personal vanity to gratify in recording the fact of my having been for many years after an associate in all the enterprises of that gallant band, I consider it more particularly a duty which every military writer owes to posterity, (be his pretensions great or humble,) to shew what may be effected in that profession by diligence and perseverance.

The light division, and the cavalry attached to it, was at this period so far in advance of every other part of the army that their safety depended on themselves alone, for they were altogether beyond the reach of human aid—their force consisted of about four thousand infantry, twelve hundred cavalry, and a brigade of horse artillery—and yet with this small force did Crawfurd, trusting to his own admirable arrangements, and the surprising discipline of his troops, maintain a position which was no position, for three months, within an hour's march of six thousand horsemen, and two hours' march from sixty thousand infantry, of a brave, experienced, and enterprising enemy, who was advancing in the confidence of certain victory.

Napier says, " His situation demanded a " quickness and intelligence in the troops, the

" like of which has seldom been known. Seven
" minutes sufficed for the division to get under
" arms in the middle of the night, and a quarter
" of an hour, night or day, to bring it in
" order of battle to the alarm posts, with the
" baggage loaded and assembled at a convenient
" distance in the rear. And this not upon a
" concerted signal, or as a trial, but at all
" times, and certain !"

" In peace love tunes the shepherd's reed ;
   In war he mounts the warrior's steed."

And thus, in humble imitation of her master-
man, did Mother Coleman, one fine morning,
mount her donkey, and join her French lover to
war against her lord.

While the troops of the light division, as
already noticed, were strutting about with the
consciousness of surpassing excellence, menacing and insulting a foe for which their persons'
knapsacks and all would barely have sufficed
for a luncheon—a dish of mortification was
served up for those of our corps, by the hands

of their better half, which was not easy of digestion. To speak of the wife of a regiment is so very unusual as to imply that she must have been some very great personage—and without depriving her of the advantage of such a magnificent idea, I shall only say that she was the only wife they had got—for they landed at Lisbon with eleven hundred men and only one woman.

By what particular virtues she had attained such a dignified position among them, I never clearly made out, further than that she had arrived at years of discretion, was what is commonly called a useful woman, and had seen some service. She was the wife of a sturdy German, who plied in the art of shoemaking, whenever his duties in the field permitted him to resort to that species of amusement, so that it appeared that she had beauty enough to captivate a cobbler, she had money enough to command the services of a jackass, and finally she proved she had wit enough to sell us all, which she did the first favourable opportunity—for, after plying for some months at the tail of her donkey at the tail of the regiment, and fishing in all the loose dollars which were floating about in gentlemen's pockets, (by those winning ways which ladies know so well how to use when such favourable opportunities offer,) she finally bolted off to the enemy, bag and baggage, carrying away old Coleman's all and awl.

It was one of those French leave-takings which man is heir to, but we eventually got over it, under the deepest obligation all the time for the sympathy manifested by our friends of the 43d and 52d.

The movements of the enemy were at length unshackled by the fall of Ciudad Rodrigo, after a desperate defence, which gave immortal glory to its old governor Herrasti, and his brave Spanish garrison—and although it may appear that I am saying one word in honour of the Spaniards for the purpose of giving two to the British, yet my feelings are too national to permit me to pass over a fact which redounds so much to the glory of our military history—namely, that in this, the year 1810, the French were six weeks in wresting from the Spaniards the same fortress which we, in the year 1812, carried, with fire and sword, out of the hands of the French in eleven days!

Now that the enemy's movements were unshackled, the cloud, which for months had been gathering over Portugal, began to burst—and, sharp as Crawfurd and his division looked before, it now behoved them to look somewhat sharper. Had he acted in conformity with his instructions, he had long ere this been behind the Coa, but deeply enamoured of his separate command as ever youth was of his mistress, he seemed resolved that nothing but force should part them; and having gradually given ground, as necessity compelled, the 23d of July found him with his back on the river, and his left resting on the fortress of Almeida, determined to abide a battle, with about five thousand men of all arms to oppose the whole French army.

I shall leave to abler pens the description of the action that followed, and which (as might have

been foreseen, while it was highly honourable
to the officers and troops engaged) ended in
their being driven across the Coa with a severe
loss. My business is with a youth who had the
day before joined the division. The history of
his next day's adventure has beguiled me of
many a hearty laugh, and although I despair of
being able to communicate it to my readers with
any thing like the humour with which I received
it from an amiable and gallant friend, yet I
cannot resist giving it such as it rests on my
remembrance.

Mr. Rogers, as already stated, had, the day
before, arrived from England, as an officer of
one of the civil departments attached to the
light division, and as might be expected on finding himself all at once up with the outposts of
the army, he was full of curiosity and excitement. Equipped in a huge cocked hat, and a
hermaphrodite sort of scarlet coat, half military
and half civil, he was dancing about with his
budget of inquiries, when chance threw him in
the way of the gallant and lamented Jock

Mac Culloch, at the time a lieutenant in the
Rifles, and who was in the act of marching off
a company to relieve one of the picquets for the
night.

Mac Culloch, full of humour, seeing the curiosity of the fresh arrival, said, " Come, Rogers,
my boy, come along with me, you shall share
my beefsteak, you shall share my boat-cloak,
and it will go hard with me but you shall
see a Frenchman, too, before we part in the
morning."

The invitation was not to be resisted, and
away went Rogers on the spur of the moment.

The night turned out a regular Tam o'Shanter's night, or, if the reader pleases, a Wellington night, for it is a singular fact that
almost every one of his battles was preceded by
such a night;—the thunder rolled, the lightning flashed, and all the fire-engines in the
world seemed playing upon the lightning, and
the devoted heads of those exposed to it. It
was a sort of night that was well calculated to
be a damper to a bolder spirit than the one

whose story I am relating; but he, nevertheless, sheltered himself as he best could, under the veteran's cloak, and put as good a face upon it as circumstances would permit.

As usual, an hour before day-break, Mac Culloch, resigning the boat-cloak to his dosing companion, stood to his arms, to be ready for whatever changes daylight might have in store for him : nor had he to wait long, for day had just begun to dawn when the sharp crack from the rifle of one of the advanced sentries announced the approach of the enemy, and he had just time to counsel his terrified bedfellow to make the best of his way back to the division, while he himself awaited to do battle. Nor had he much time for preparation, for, as Napier says, " Ney, seeing Crawfurd's false dispositions, came down upon them with the stoop of an eagle. Four thousand horsemen, and a powerful artillery, swept the plain, and Loison's division coming up at a charging pace, made towards the centre and left of the position." Mac Culloch, almost instantly, received several bad sabre wounds, and, with five-and-twenty of his men, was taken prisoner.

Rogers, it may be believed, lost no time in following the salutary counsel he had received with as clever a pair of heels as he could muster. The enemy's artillery had by this time opened, and, as the devil would have it, the cannon-balls were travelling the same road, and tearing up the ground on each side of him almost as regularly as if it had been a ploughing match. Poor Rogers was thus placed in a situation which fully justified him in thinking, as most young soldiers do, that every ball was aimed at himself. He was half distracted; it was certain death to stop where he was, neither flank offered him the smallest shelter, and he had not wind enough left in his bellows to clear the tenth part of the space between him and comparative safety; but, where life is at stake, the imagination is fertile, and it immediately occurred to him that by dowsing the cocked hat he would make himself a less conspicuous object; clapping it, accord-

ingly under his arm, he continued his frightful
career, with the feelings of a maniac and the
politeness of a courtier, for to every missile that
passed he bowed as low as his racing attitude
would permit, in ignorance that the danger had
passed along with it, performing, to all appearance, a continued rotatory sort of evolution, as
if the sails of a windmill had parted from the
building, and continued their course across the
plain, to the utter astonishment of all who saw
him. At length, when exhausted nature could
not have carried him twenty yards further, he
found himself among some skirmishers of the
3d Caçadores, and within a few yards of a rocky
ridge, rising out of the ground, the rear of
which seemed to offer him the long-hoped-for
opportunity of recovering his wind, and he sheltered himself accordingly.

This happened to be the first occasion in which
the Caçadores had been under fire; they had the
highest respect for the bravery of their British
officers, and had willingly followed where their
colonel had led; but having followed him into

the field, they did not see why they should not
follow another out of it, and when they saw a
red coat take post behind a rock, they all immediately rushed to take advantage of the same
cover. Poor Rogers had not, therefore, drawn
his first breath when he found himself surrounded by these Portuguese warriors, nor had
he drawn a second before their colonel (Sir
George Elder) rode furiously at him with his
drawn sword, exclaiming " who are you, you
scoundrel, in the uniform of a British officer, setting an example of cowardice to my
men ? get out of that instantly, or I'll cut you
down !"

Rogers's case was desperate—he had no breath
left to explain that he had no pretensions to the
honour of being an officer, for he would have
been cut down in the act of attempting it : he
was, therefore, once more forced to start for
another heat with the round shot, and, like a
hunted devil, got across the bridge, he knew
not how ; but he was helm up for England the
same day, and the army never saw him more.

General Crawfurd's conduct in the affair alluded to, would argue that his usual soldier-
like wits had gone a wool-gathering for the time
being—he had, in fact, like a moth, been fluttering so long with impunity around a consuming
power that he had at length lost all sense of the
danger. But even then it is impossible to con-
ceive upon what principle he took up the position he did—for, in the first place, it was in
direct defiance of Lord Wellington's orders ; and
had the river behind him been flowing with milk
and honey, or had the rugged bank on which
he was posted been built of loaves and fishes, it
would scarcely have justified him in running the
risk he did to preserve the sweets ; but as the
one was flooded with muddy water, and the
other only bearing a crop of common stones,
and when we consider, too, that the simple
passing of the river would have made a hundred
of his troops equal to a thousand of the invaders,
we must continue lost in wonder.

It is difficult to imagine, however, that he
ever contemplated the possibility of stopping the

French army but for the moment. Confiding, probably, in the superiority of his troops, he had calculated on successfully repelling their first attack, and that having thus taught them the respect that was due to him, he might then have made a triumphant retreat to the opposite bank, where, for a time, he could safely have offered them further defiance.

If such was his object, (and it is the only plausible one I can find,) he had altogether overlooked that for a man with one pair of arms to grapple with another who had ten, it must rest with the ten-pair man to say when the play is over, for although the one-pair man may disable an equal number in his front, there are still nine pair left to poke him in the sides and all round about; and thus the general found it; for having once exposed himself to such overwhelming numbers, there was no getting out of it but at a large sacrifice—and but for the experience, the confidence, and the devotion of the different individual battalion officers, seconded by the gallantry of the soldiers, the division had been utterly annihilated. Napier, as an eye-witness, states, (what I have often heard repeated by other officers who were there,) that " there " was no room to array the line, no time for " any thing but battle, every captain carried off " his company as an independent body, and " joining as he could with the ninety-fifth or " fifty-second, the whole presented a mass of " skirmishers acting in small parties, and under " no regular command, yet each confident in " the courage and discipline of those on his " right and left, and all regulating their move-" ments by a common discretion, and keeping " together with surprising vigour."

The result of the action was a loss on the British portion of the division of two hundred and seventy-two, including twenty-eight officers, killed, wounded, and taken.

It is curious to observe by what singular interpositions of Providence the lives of individuals are spared. One of our officers happening to have a pocket-volume of Gil Blas, was in the middle of one of his interesting stories when the action commenced. Not choosing to throw it away, he thrust it into the breast of his jacket for want of a better place, and in the course of the day it received a musket-ball which had been meant for a more tender subject. The volume was afterwards, of course, treated as a tried friend.

Having, in one of the foregoing pages, introduced the name of Mac Culloch in a prominent part of the action, I must be forgiven for taking this opportunity of following him to the end of his highly honourable earthly career.

John Mac Culloch was from Scotland, (a native, I believe, of Kirkudbright;) he was young, handsome, athletic, and active; with the meekness of a lamb, he had the heart of a lion, and was the delight of every one. At the time I first became acquainted with him he had been several years in the regiment, and had shared in all the vicissitudes of the restless life they then led. I brought him under the notice of the reader in marching off to relieve the advanced picquet on the night prior to the action of the Coa.

For the information of those who are unacquainted with military matters, I may as well
mention that the command of an outline picquet
is never an enviable one—it is a situation at all
times dangerous and open to disgrace, but seldom to honour—for come what may, in the event
of an attack spiritedly made, the picquet is
almost sure to go to the wall.   From the manner
in which the French approached on the occasion
referred to, it may readily be imagined that my
gallant friend had but little chance of escape—
it was, therefore, only left to him to do his duty
as an officer under the circumstances in which
he was placed. He gave the alarm, and he
gave his visitors as warm a reception as his fifty
rifles could provide for them, while he gallantly
endeavoured to fight his way back to his battalion, but the attempt was hopeless ; the cavalry
alone of the enemy ought to have been more
than enough to sweep the whole of the division
off the face of the earth—and Mac Culloch's small
party had no chance ; they were galloped into,

and he, himself, after being lanced and sabred in many places, was obliged to surrender.

Mac Culloch refused to give his parole, in the hope of being able to effect his escape before he reached the French frontier; he was, therefore, marched along with the men a close prisoner as far as Valladolid, where fortune, which ever favours the brave, did not fail him. The escort had found it necessary to halt there for some days, and Mac Culloch having gained the goodwill of his conductor, was placed in a private house under proper security, as they thought; but in this said house there happened to be a young lady, and of what avail are walls of brass, bolts, bars, or iron doors, when a lady is concerned? She quickly put herself in communion with the handsome prisoner—made herself acquainted with his history, name, and country, and as quickly communicated it, as well as her plans for his escape, to a very worthy countryman of his, at that time a professor in one of the universities there. Need I say more than that before many hours had passed over

his head, he found himself equipped in the costume of a Spanish peasant, the necessary quantity of dollars in his pocket, and a kiss on each
cheek burning hot from the lips of his preserver,
on the high road to rejoin his battalion, where
he arrived in due course of time, to the great
joy of every body—Lord Wellington himself
was not the least delighted of the party, and
kindly invited him to dine with him that day, in
the *costume* in which he had arrived.

Mac Culloch continued to serve with us until
Massena's retreat from Portugal, when, in a
skirmish which took place on the evening of the
15th of March, 1811, I, myself, got a crack
on the head which laid me under a tree, with
my understanding considerably bothered for the
night, and I was sorry to find, as my next
neighbour, poor Mac Culloch, with an excru-
ciatingly painful and bad wound in the shoulder
joint, which deprived him of the use of one arm
for life, and obliged him to return to England
for the recovery of health.

In the meantime, by the regular course of

promotion, he received his company, which transferred him to the 2d battalion, and, serving with it at the battle of Waterloo, he lost his sound arm by one of the last shots that was fired in that bloody field.

As soon as he had recovered from this last wound he rejoined us in Paris, and, presenting himself before the Duke of Wellington in his usual straightforward manly way, said, " Here I " am, my Lord; I have no longer an arm left " to wield for my country, but I still wish to " be allowed to serve it as I best can !" The Duke duly appreciated the diamond before him, and as there were several captains in the regiment senior to Mac Culloch, his Grace, with due regard to their feelings, desired the commanding officer to ascertain whether they would not consider it a cause of complaint if Mac Culloch were recommended for a brevet majority, as it was out of his power to do it for every one, and, to the honour of all concerned, there was not a dissentient voice. He, therefore, succeeded to the brevet, and was afterwards promoted to a majority, I think, in a veteran battalion.

He was soon after on a visit in London, living at a hotel, when one afternoon he was taken suddenly ill; the feeling to him was an unusual one, and he immediately sent for a physician, and told him that he cared not for the consequences, but insisted on having his candid opinion on his case.

The medical man accordingly told him at once that his case was an extraordinary one—that he might within an hour or two recover from it, or within an hour or two he might be no more.

Mac Culloch, with his usual coolness, gave a few directions as to the future, and calmly awaited the result, which terminated fatally within the time predicted—and thus perished, in the prime of life, the gallant Mac Culloch, who was alike an honour to his country and his profession.

CHAP. V.

The paying of a French compliment, which will be repaid
in a future chapter. A fierce attack upon hairs. A niece
compliment, and lessons gratis to untaught sword-bearers.

AFTER the action of the Coa the enemy quickly
possessed themselves of the fortress of Almeida,
when there remained nothing between Massena
and his kingdom but the simple article of Lord
Wellington's army, of which he calculated he
would be able to superintend the embarkation
within the time requisite for his infantry to
march to Lisbon. He therefore put his legions
in motion to pay his distinguished adversary
that last mark of respect.

The Wellingtonians retired slowly before them
shewing their teeth as often as favourable oppor-

tunities offered, and several bitter bites they
gave before they turned at bay—first on the
heights of Busaco, and finally and effectually
on those of Torres Vedras.

The troops of all arms composing the rear
guard conducted themselves admirably throughout the whole of that retreat, for although the
enemy did not press them so much as they
might have done, yet they were at all times in
close contact, and many times in actual combat,
and it was impossible to say which was the most
distinguished—the splendid service of the horse
artillery, the dashing conduct of the dragoons,
or the unconquerable steadiness and bravery of
the infantry.

It was a sort of military academy which is
not open for instruction every day in the year,
nor was it one which every fond mamma would
choose to send her darling boy to, calculated
although it was to lead to *immortal* honours.
A youngster (if he did not stop a bullet by the
way) might commence his studies in such a
place with nothing but " the soft down peeping

through the white skin," and be entitled to the respect due to a beard or a bald head before he saw the end of it.

It is curious to remark how fashions change and how the change affects the valour of the man too. The dragoon since the close of the war has worn all his hair below the head and none on the top it, and how fiercely he fought in defence of his whiskers the other day when some of the regiments were ordered to be shaved, as if the debility of Samson was likely to be the result of the operation. My stars! but I should be glad to know what the old royal *heavies* or fourteenth and sixteenth *lights* cared about hairs at the period I speak of, when with their bare faces they went boldly in and bearded muzzles that seemed fenced with furze bushes; and while it was " damned be he who first cries hold — enough !" they did hold enough too, sometimes bringing in every man his bird, mustachoes and all. In those days they seemed to put more faith in their good right hand than in a cart-load of whiskers, for with it and their open English countenances they carved for themselves a name as British dragoons, which they were too proud to barter for any other.

Every attempt at rearing a *moustache* among the British in those days was treated with sovereign contempt, no matter how aristocratic the soil on which it was sown. But, to do justice to *every body*, I must say that, to the best of my recollection, a crop was seldom seen but on the lips of *nobodies*.

It was in the course of this retreat, as I mentioned in a former work, that I first joined Lord Wellington's army, and I remember being remarkably struck with the order, the confidence, and the daring spirit which seemed to animate all ranks of those among whom it was my good fortune to be cast. Their confidence in their illustrious chief was unbounded, and they seemed to feel satisfied that it only rested with him any day to say to his opponent, " thus far shalt thou come but no farther ;" and if a doubt on the subject had rested with any one before, the battle of Busaco removed it, for the Portuguese troops having succeeded in beating their man, it confirmed them in their own good opinion, and gave increased confidence to the whole allied army.

I am now treading on the heels of my former narrative, and although it did not include the field of Busaco, yet, as I have already stated, it is foreign to my present purpose to enter into any details of the actions in which we were engaged, further than they may serve to illustrate such anecdotes as appear to me to be likely to amuse the reader. I shall therefore pass over the present one, merely remarking that to a military man, one of the most interesting spectacles which took place there, was the light division taking up their ground the day before in the face of the enemy. They had remained too long in their advanced position on the morning of the 25th of September while the enemy's masses were gathering around them; but Lord Wellington fortunately came up before they were too far committed and put them in immediate retreat under his own personal direction. Nor,

as Napier says, " Was there a moment to lose,
" for the enemy with incredible rapidity brought
" up both infantry and guns, and fell on so
" briskly that all the skill of the general and
" the readiness of the excellent troops com-
" posing the rear guard, could scarcely prevent
" the division from being dangerously engaged.
" Howbeit, a series of rapid and beautiful
" movements, a sharp cannonade, and an hour's
" march, brought every thing back in good
" order to the great position."

On the day of the battle (the 27th) the
French General Simon, who led the attack upon
our division, was wounded and taken prisoner,
and as they were bringing him in he raved
furiously for General Crawfurd, daring him to
single combat, but as he was already a prisoner
there would have been but little wit in indulging
him in his humour.

In the course of the afternoon his baggage
was brought in under a flag of truce, accompanied by a charm to soothe the savage breast,
in the shape of a very beautiful little Spanish

girl, who I have no doubt succeeded in tran-
quillizing his pugnacious disposition. I know
not what rank she held on his establishment, but
conclude that she was his niece, for I have
observed that in Spain the prettiest girl in every
gentleman's house is the niece. The Padrès
particularly are the luckiest fellows in the
world in having the handsomest brothers and
sisters of any men living,—not that I have seen
the brother or the sister of any one of them,
but then I have seen nine hundred and ninety-
nine Padrès, and each had his niece at the head
of his establishment, and I know not how it
happened but she was always the prettiest girl in
the parish.

It was generally the fate of troops arriving
from England, to join the army at an unhappy
period—at a time when easy stages and refreshment after the voyage was particularly wanted
and never to be had. The marches at this
period were harassing and severe, and the company with which I had just arrived were much distressed to keep pace with the old campaigners—

they made a tolerable scramble for a day or two, but by the time they arrived at the lines the greater part had been obliged to be mounted. Nevertheless, when it became Massena's turn to tramp out of Portugal a few months after, we found them up to their work and with as few stragglers as the best. Marching is an art to be acquired only by habit, and one in which the strength or agility of the animal, man, has but little to do. I have seen Irishmen (and all sorts of countrymen) in their own country, taken from the plough-tail—huge, athletic, active fellows, who would think nothing of doing forty or fifty miles in the course of the day as countrymen—see these men placed in the rank as recruits with knapsacks on their backs and a musket over their shoulders, and in the first march they are dead beat before they get ten miles.

I have heard many disputes on the comparative campaigning powers of tall and short men, but as far as my own experience goes I have never seen any difference. If a tall man hap-

pens to break down it is immediately noticed to
the disadvantage of his class, but if the same
misfortune befals a short one, it is not looked
upon as being anything remarkable. The effective powers of both in fact depend upon the
nature of the building.

The most difficult and at the same time the
most important duty to teach a young soldier on
first coming into active service, is how to take
care of himself. It is one which, in the first
instance, requires the unwearied attention of the
officer, but he is amply repaid in the long run,
for when the principle is once instilled into him,
it is duly appreciated, and he requires no further
trouble. In our battalion, during the latter years
of the war, it was a mere matter of form in-
specting the men on parade, for they knew too
well the advantages of having their arms and
ammunition at all times in proper order to neglect them, so that after several weeks marching
and fighting, I have never seen them on their
first ordinary parade after their arrival in quarters,
but they were fit for the most rigid examination

of the greatest Martinet that ever looked through the ranks. The only thing that required the officers' attention was their necessaries, for as money was scarce, they were liable to be bartered for strong waters.

On service as every where else, there is a time for all things, but the time there being limited and very uncertain, the difficulty is to learn how to make the most of it.

The first and most important part lies with the officer, and he cannot do better than borrow a leaf out of General Crawfurd's book, to learn how to prevent straggling, and to get his men to the end of their day's work with the least possible delay.

The young soldier when he first arrives in camp or bivouac will (unless forced to do otherwise) always give in to the languor and fatigue which oppresses him, and fall asleep. He awakens most probably after dark, cold and comfortless. He would gladly eat some of the undressed meat in his haversack, but he has no fire on which to cook it. He would gladly

shelter himself in one of the numerous huts
which have arisen around him since he fell
asleep, but as he lent no hand in the building
he is thrust out. He attempts at the eleventh
hour to do as others have done, but the time
has gone by, for all the materials that were
originally within reach, have already been ap-
propriated by his more active neighbours, and
there is nothing left for him but to pass the
remainder of the night as he best can, in hunger,
in cold, and in discomfort, and he marches
before day-light in the morning without having
enjoyed either rest or refreshment. Such is
often the fate of young regiments for a longer
period than would be believed, filling the hos-
pitals and leading to all manner of evils.

On the other hand, see the old soldiers come
to their ground. Let their feelings of fatigue be
great or small, they are no sooner suffered to
leave the ranks than every man rushes to secure
whatever the neighbourhood affords as likely to
contribute towards his comfort for the night.
Swords, hatchets, and bill-kooks are to be seen

hewing and hacking at every tree and bush
within reach,—huts are quickly reared, fires are
quickly blazing, and while the camp kettle is
boiling, or the pound of beef frying, the tired,
but happy souls, are found toasting their toes
around the cheerful blaze, recounting their
various adventures until the fire has done the
needful, when they fall on like men, taking
especial care however that whatever their inclinations may be, they consume no part of the
provision which properly belongs to the morrow.
The meal finished, they arrange their accoutrements in readiness for any emergency, (caring
little for the worst that can befal them for the
next twenty-four hours,) when they dispose
themselves for rest, and be their allowance of
sleep long or short they enjoy it, for it does
one's heart good to see " the rapture of repose
that's there."

In actual battle, young soldiers are apt to
have a feeling, (from which many old ones are
not exempt,) namely, that they are but insignificant characters—only a humble individual out

of many thousands, and that his conduct, be it good or bad, can have little influence over the fate of the day. This is a monstrous mistake, which it ought to be the duty of every military writer to endeavour to correct; for in battle, as elsewhere, no man is insignificant unless he chooses to make himself so. The greater part of the victories on record, I believe, may be traced to the individual gallantry of a very small portion of the troops engaged; and if it were possible to take a microscopic view of that small portion, there is reason to think that the whole of the glory might be found to rest with a very few individuals.

Military men in battle may be classed under three disproportionate heads,—a very small class who consider themselves insignificant— a very large class who content themselves with doing their duty, without going beyond it—and a tolerably large class who do their best, many of which are great men without knowing it. One example in the history of a private soldier will establish all that I have advanced on the subject.

In one of the first smart actions that I ever was in, I was a young officer in command of experienced soldiers, and, therefore, found my-self compelled to be an observer rather than an active leader in the scene.   We were engaged in a very hot skirmish, and had driven the enemy's light troops for a considerable distance with great rapidity, when we were at length stopped by some of their regiments in line, which open-ed such a terrific fire within a few yards that it obliged every one to shelter himself as he best could among the inequalities of the ground and the sprinkling of trees which the place afforded. We remained inactive for about ten minutes amidst a shower of balls that seemed to be almost like a hail-storm, and when at the very worst, when it appeared to me to be certain death to quit the cover, a young scampish fellow of the name of Priestly, at the adjoining tree, started out from behind it, saying, " Well ! I'll be d——d if I'll be bothered any longer behind a tree, so here's at you," and with that he banged off his rifle in the face of his foes, reloading very deliberately, while every one right and left followed his example, and the enemy, panic struck, took to their heels without firing another shot. The action requires no comment, the individual did not seem to be aware that he had any merit in what he did, but it is nevertheless a valuable example for those who are disposed to study causes and effects in the art of war.

In that same action I saw an amusing instance of the ruling passion for sport predominating over a soldier; a rifleman near me was in the act of taking aim at a Frenchman when a hare crossed between them, the muzzle of the rifle mechanically followed the hare in preference, and, as she was doubling into our lines, I had just time to strike up the piece with my sword before he drew the trigger, or he most probably would have shot one of our own people, for he was so intent upon his game that he had lost sight of every thing else.

CHAP. VI.

Reaping a Horse with a Halter. Reaping golden Opinions
out of a Dung-Hill, and reaping a good Story or two out
of the next Room. A Dog-Hunt and Sheep's Heads prepared at the Expense of a Dollar each, and a Scotchman's
Nose.

I HAVE taken so many flights from our line of
retreat in search of the fanciful, that I can only
bring my readers back to our actual position,
by repeating the oft told tale that our army
pulled up in the lines of Torres Vedras to await
Massena's further pleasure; for, whether he was
to persevere in his intended compliment of seeing us on board ship, or we were to return it by
seeing him out of Portugal again, was still somewhat doubtful; and, until the point should be

decided, we made ourselves as comfortable as circumstances would permit, and that was pretty well.

Every young officer on entering a new stage in his profession, let him fancy himself ever so acute, is sure to become for a time the *butt* of the old hands. I was the latest arrival at the time I speak of, and of course shared the fate of others, but as the only hoax that I believe they ever tried upon me, turned out a profitable one, I had less cause for soreness than falls to the lot of green-horns in general. It consisted in an officer, famous for his waggery, coming up to me one morning and mentioning that he had just been taking a ride over a part of the mountain, (which he pointed out,) where he had seen a wild horse grazing, and that he had tried hard to catch him, but lamented that he had been unable to succeed, for that he was a very handsome one!

As the country abounded in wolves and other wild characters I did not see why there should not also be wild horses, and, therefore, greedily

swallowed the bait, for I happened not only to
be in especial want of a horse, but of dollars to
buy one, and arming myself accordingly with a
halter and the assistance of an active rifleman,
I proceeded to the place, and very quickly converted the wild horse into a tame one! It was
not until a year after that I discovered the hoax
by which I had unwittingly become the stealer
of some unfortunate man's horse; but, in the
mean time, it was to the no small mortification
of my waggish friend, that he saw me mounted
upon him when we marched a few days after,
for he had anticipated a very different result.

The saddle which sat between me and the
horse on that occasion ought not to be overlooked, for, take it all in all, I never expect to see
its like again. I found it in our deserted house
at Arruda; the seat was as soft as a pillow, and
covered with crimson silk velvet, beautifully
embroidered, and gilt round the edges. I knew
not for what description of rider it had been
intended, but I can answer for it that it was
exceedingly comfortable in dry weather, and

that in wet it possessed all the good properties of a sponge, keeping the rider cool and comfortable.

While we remained in the lines, there was a small, thatched, mud-walled, deserted cottage under the hill near our company's post, which we occasionally used as a shelter from the sun or the rain, and some of our men in prowling about one day discovered two massive silver salvers concealed in the thatch. The captain of the company very properly ordered them to be taken care of, in the hope that their owner would come to claim them, while the soldiers in the mean time continued very eager in their researches in the neighbourhood, in expectation of making further discoveries, in which however they were unsuccessful. After we had altogether abandoned the cottage, a Portuguese gentleman arrived one day and told us that he was the owner of the place, and that he had some plate concealed there which he wished permission to remove. Captain ——— immediately desired the salvers to be given to him, concluding that

they were what he had come in search of, but
on looking at them he said that they did not
belong to him, that what he wished to remove
was concealed under the dunghill, and he accordingly proceeded there and dug out about a
cart load of gold and silver articles which he
carried off, while our unsuccessful searchers
stood by, cursing their mutual understandings
which had suffered such a prize to slip through
their fingers, and many an innocent heap of
manure was afterwards torn to pieces in consequence of that morning's lesson.

Massena having abandoned his desolated position in the early part of November, the fifteenth
of that month saw me seated on my cloth of
crimson and gold, taking a look at the French
rear guard, which, under Junot, was in position
between Cartaxo and El Valle. A cool November breeze whistled through an empty stomach,
which the gilded outside was insufficient to
satisfy. Our chief of division was red hot to
send us over to warm ourselves with the French
fires, and had absolutely commenced the move-

ment when the opportune arrival of Lord Wellington put a stop to it; for, as it was afterwards discovered, we should have burnt our
fingers.

While we therefore awaited further orders on
the road side, I was amused to see General
Slade, who commanded the brigade of cavalry
attached to us, order up his sumpter mule, and
borrowing our doctor's medical panniers, which
he placed in the middle of the road by way of a
table, he, with the assistance of his orderly
dragoon, undid several packages, and presently
displayed a set-out which was more than enough
to tempt the cupidity of the hungry beholders,
consisting of an honest-looking loaf of bread, a
thundering large tongue, and the fag end of a
ham—a bottle of porter, and half a one of
brandy. The bill of fare is still as legibly written
on my remembrance as on the day that I first
saw it—for such things cannot be, and overcome
us like the vision of a Christmas feast, without
especial longings for an invitation; but we might
have sighed and looked, and sighed again, for

our longings were useless—our doctor, with his
usual politeness, made sundry attempts to in-
sinuate himself upon the hospitable notice of
the general, by endeavouring to arrange the
panniers in a more classical shape for his better
accommodation, for which good service he received bow for bow, with a considerable quantity of thanks into the bargain, which, after he
had done his best, (and that was no joke,) still
left him the general's debtor on the score of
civility.   When the doctor had failed, the attempt of any other individual became a forlorn
hope, but nothing seems desperate to a British
soldier, and two thorough going ones, the commanders of the twelfth and fourteenth light
dragoons, (Colonels Ponsonby and Harvey,)
whose olfactory nerves, at a distance of some
hundred yards, having snuffed up the tainted
air, eagerly followed the scent, and came to a
dead point before the general and his panniers.
But although they had flushed their game they
did not succeed in bagging it; for while the
general gave them plenty of his own tongue,

the deuce take the slice did he offer of the
bullock's—and as soon as he had satisfied his
appetite he very deliberately bundled up the
fragments, and shouted to horse, for the enemy
had by this time withdrawn from our front, and
joined the main body of the army on the heights
of Santarem. We closed up to them, and exchanged a few civil shots—a ceremony which
cannot be dispensed with between contending
armies on first taking up their ground, for it
defines their territorial rights, and prevents
future litigation.

Day-light next morning showed that, though
they had passed a restless night, they were not
disposed to extend their walk unless compelled
to it, for their position, formidable by nature,
had, by their unwearied activity, become more
so by art—the whole crest of it being already
fenced with an abbatis of felled trees, and the
ground turned up in various directions.

One of our head-quarter staff-officers came to
take a look at them in the early part of the
morning, and, assuming a superior knowledge

of all that was passing, said that they had nothing there but a rear-guard, and that we should shove them from it in the course of the day—upon which, our brigadier, (Sir Sidney Beckwith,) who had already scanned every thing with his practised eye, dryly remarked, in his usual homely but emphatic language, " It was a gay strong rear guard that built that abbatis last night !" And so it proved, for their whole army had been employed in its construction, and there they remained for the next four months.

The company to which I belonged, (and another,) had a deserted farming establishment turned over for our comfort and convenience during the period that it might suit the French marshal to leave us in the enjoyment thereof. It was situated on a slope of the hill overlooking the bridge of Santarem, and within range of the enemy's sentries, and near the end of it was one of the finest aloes I have ever seen, certainly not less than twelve or fourteen feet high. Our mansion was a long range of common thatched

building—one end was a kitchen—next to it a
parlour, which became also the drawing and
sleeping room of two captains, with their six
jolly subs—a door-way communicated from
thence to the barn, which constituted the greater
part of the range, and lodged our two hundred
men. A small apartment at the other extremity, which was fitted up for a wine-press,
lodged our non-commissioned officers; while
in the back-ground we had accommodation for
our cattle, and for sundry others of the domestic
tribes, had we had the good fortune to be furnished with them.

The door-way between the officers' apartment
and that of the soldiers showed, (what is so
very common on the seat of war,) when " a
door is not a door," but a shovel full of dust
and ashes—the hinges had resisted manfully by
clinging to the door-post, but a fiery end had
overtaken the timber, and we were obliged to
fill up the vacuum with what loose stones we
could collect in the neighbourhood; it was,
nevertheless, so open, that a hand might be

thrust through it in every direction, and, of course, the still small voices on either side of the partition were alike audible to all. I know not what degree of amusement the soldiers derived from the proceedings on our side of the wall, but I know that the jests, the tales, and the songs, from their side, constituted our greatest enjoyment during the many long winter nights that it was our fate to remain there.

The early part of their evenings was generally spent in witticisms and tales; and, in conclusion, by way of a lullaby, some long-winded fellow commenced one of those everlasting ditties in which soldiers and sailors delight so much —they are all to the same tune, and the subject, (if one may judge by the tenor of the first ninety-eight verses,) was battle, murder, or sudden death; but I never yet survived until the catastrophe, although I have often, to attain that end, stretched my waking capacities to the utmost. I have sometimes heard a fresh arrival from England endeavour to astonish their unpolished ears with " the white blossomed sloe," or some such refined melody, but it was invariably coughed down as instantaneously as if it had been the sole voice of a conservative amidst a select meeting of radicals.

The wit and the humour of the rascals were amusing beyond any thing—and to see them next morning drawn up as mute as mice, and as stiff as lamp-posts, it was a regular puzzler to discover on which *post* the light had shone during the bye-gone night, knowing, as we did, that there were at least a hundred original pages for Joe Miller, encased within the head-pieces then before us.

Their stories, too, were quite unique—one, (an Englishman,) began detailing the unfortunate termination of his last matrimonial speculation. He had got a pass one day to go from Shorncliffe to Folkestone, and on the way he fell in with one of the finest young women " as ever he seed ! my eye, as we say in Spain, if she was not a *wapper ;* with a pair of cheeks like cherries, and shanks as clean as my ramrod, she was bounding over the downs like a young colt,

and faith, if she would not have been with her
heels clean over my head if I had'n't caught
her up and demanded a parley.   O, Jem, man,
but she was a nice creature ! and all at once got
so fond of me too, that there was no use waiting ; and so we settled it all that self same
night, and on the next morning we were regularly spliced, and I carries her home to a hut
which Corporal Smith and I hired behind the
barrack for eighteen pence a week.   Well ! I'll
be blessed if I was'n't as happy as a shilling a
day and my wife could make me for two whole
days ; but the next morning, just before parade,
while Nancy was toasting a slice of tommy*
for our breakfast, who should darken our door
but the carcase of a great sea marine, who began blinking his goggle eyes like an owl in a
gooseberry bush, as if he did'n't see nothing
outside on them ; when all at once Nancy turned, and, my eye, what a squall she set up as
she threw the toast in the fire, and upset my

* Brown loaf.

tinful of crowdy, while she twisted her arms
round his neck like a vice, and began kissing
him at no rate, he all the time blubbering, like a
bottle-nose in a shoal, about flesh of his flesh,
and bones of his bones, and all the like o' that.
Well! says I to myself, says I, this is very
queer any how—and then I eyes the chap a bit,
and then says I to him, (for I began to feel
somehow at seeing my wife kissed all round before my face without saying by your leave,) an'
says I to him, (rather angrily,) look ye, Mr.
Marine, if you don't take your ugly mouth farther off from my wife, I'll just punch it with the
butt end of my rifle! thunder and oons, you
great sea lobster that you are, don't you see that
I married her only two days ago just as she
stands, bones and all, and you to come at this
time o' day to claim a part on her!"

The marine, however, had come from the
wars as a man of peace—he had already been
at her father's, and learnt all that had befallen
her, and, in place of provoking the rifleman's

further ire, he sought an amicable explanation,
which was immediately entered into.

It appeared that Nancy and he had been married some three years before; that the sloop of
war to which he belonged was ordered to the
West Indies, and while cruising on that station an unsuccessful night attempt was made
to cut out an enemy's craft from under a battery,
in the course of which the boat in which he was
embarked having been sent to the bottom with a
thirty-two pound shot, he was supposed to have
gone along with it, and to be snugly reposing in
Davy Jones's locker. His present turn up, however, proved his going down to have been a mistake, as he had succeeded in saving his life at
the expense of his liberty, for the time being; but
the vessel, on her voyage to France, was captured by a British frigate bound for India, and
the royal marine became once more the servant
of his lawful sovereign.

In the meanwhile Nancy had been duly ap-
prised of his supposed fate by some of his West

Indian shipmates—she was told that she might still hope; but Nancy had no idea of holding on by any thing so precarious—she was the wife of a sailor, had been frequently on board a ship, and had seen how arbitrarily every thing, even time itself, is made subservient to their purposes, and she determined to act upon the same principle, so that, as the first lieutenant authorizes it to be eight o'clock after the officer of the watch has reported that it is so, in like manner did Nancy, when her husband was reported dead, order that he should be so; but it would appear that her commands had about as much influence over her husband's fate as the first lieutenant's had over time, from his making his untoward appearance so early in her second honey-moon.

As brevity formed no part of the narrator's creed, I have merely given an outline of the marine's history, such as I understood it, and shall hasten to the conclusion in the same manner.

The explanation over, a long silence ensued—
each afraid to pop the question, which must be
popp'd, of whose wife was Nancy? and when,
at last, it did come out, it was more easily asked
than answered, for, notwithstanding all that had
passed, they continued both to be deeply enamoured of their mutual wife, and she of both,
nor could a voluntary resignation be extracted
from either of them, so that they were eventually obliged to trust the winning or the losing
of that greatest of all earthly blessings, (a beloved wife,) to the undignified decision of the
toss of a halfpenny. The marine won, and
carried off the prize—while the rifleman declared
that he had never yet forgiven himself for being
cheated out of his half, for he feels convinced
that the marine. had come there prepared with
a ha'penny that had two tails.

The tail of the foregoing story was caught up
by a *Patlander* with—" Well ! the devil fetch
me if I would have let her gone that way any
how, if the marine had brought twenty tails

with his ha'penny!—but you see I was kicked out of the only wife I never had without ere a chance of being married at all.

" Kitty, you see, was an apprentice to Miss Crump, who keeps that thundering big milliner's shop in Sackville-street, and I was Mike Kinahan's boy at the next door—so you see, whenever it was Kitty's turn to carry out one of them great blue boxes with thingumbobs for the ladies, faith, I always contrived to steal away for a bit, to give Kitty a lift, and the darling looked so kind and so grateful for't that I was at last quite kilt!"

I must here take up the thread of Paddy's story for the same reasons given in the last, and inform the reader that, though he himself had received the finishing blow, he was far from satisfied that Kitty's case was equally desperate, for, notwithstanding her grateful looks, they continued to be more like those of a mistress to an obliging servant than of a sweetheart. As for a kiss, he could not get any thing like one even by coaxing, and the greatest bliss he experienced, in the course of his love making, was in the interchange among the fingers which the frequent transfer of the band-box permitted, and which Pat declared went quite through and through him.

Matters, however, were far from keeping pace with Paddy's inclinations, and feeling convinced at last, that there must be a rival in the case, he determined to watch her very closely, in order to have his suspicions removed, or, if confirmed, to give his rival such a pounding as should prevent his ever crossing his path again. Accordingly, seeing her one evening leave the shop better dressed than usual, he followed at a distance, until opposite the post-office, when he saw her joined, (evidently by appointment,) by a tall well-dressed spalpeen of a fellow, and they then proceeded at a smart pace up the adjoining street—Paddy followed close behind in the utmost indignation, but before he had time to make up his mind as to which of his rival's bones he should begin by breaking, they all at once turned into a doorway, which Paddy found belonged to one of those dancing shops so common in Dublin.

Determined not to be foiled in that manner, and ascertaining that a decent suit of *toggery* and five *tin*-pennies in his pocket would ensure him a *free* admission, he lost no time in equipping in his Sunday's best, and having succeeded in *borrowing* the needful for the occasion out of his master's till, he sallied forth bent on conquest.

Paddy was ushered up stairs into the ballroom with all due decorum, but that commodity took leave of him at the door, for the first thing he saw on entering, was his mistress and his rival, within a yard of him, whirling in the mazes of a country dance. Pat's philosophy was unequal to the sight, and throwing one arm round the young lady's waist, and giving her partner a douse in the chops with the other, it made as satisfactory a change in their relative positions as he could have reasonably desired, by sending his rival in a continuation of his waltzing movement, to the extremity of the room to salute the wall at the end of it.

Pat, however, was allowed but brief space to congratulate himself on his successful *debut* in a ball-room, for in the next instant he found himself most ungracefully propelled through the door-way, by sundry unseen hands, which had grasped him tightly by the *scruff* of the neck, and on reaching the top of the staircase, he felt as if a hundred feet had given a simultaneous kick which raised him like a balloon for a short distance, and then away he went heels over head towards the bottom. It so happened at this particular moment, that three gentlemen very sprucely dressed, had just paid their money and were in the act of ascending, taking that opportunity, as gentlemen generally do, of arranging their hair and adjusting their frills to make their *entré* the more bewitching, and it is therefore unnecessary to say that the descent of our aëronaut not only disturbed the economy of their wigs but carried all three to the bottom with the impetus of three sacks of potatoes.

Paddy's temperament had somewhat exceeded madman's heat before he commenced his aërial flight, and, as may be imagined, it had not much cooled in its course, so that when he found himself safely landed, and, as luck would have it, on the top of one of the unfortunates, he very unceremoniously began taking the change out of his head for all the disasters of the night, and having quickly demolished the nose and bunged up both eyes, he (seeing nothing more to be done thereabouts) next proceeded to pound the unfortunate fellow's head against the floor, before they succeeded in lugging him off to finish his love adventure in the watch-house.

That night was the last of Paddy's love and of his adventures in the City of Dublin. His friends were respectable of their class, and on the score of his former good conduct, succeeded in appeasing the aggrieved parties and inducing them to withdraw from the prosecution on condition that he quitted the city for ever, and, when he had time to reflect on the position in which the reckless doings of the few hours had placed him, he was but too happy to subscribe to it, and passing over to Liverpool enlisted with a recruiting party of ours, and became an admirable soldier.

Having given two of the soldiers' stories, it may probably be amusing to my readers to hear one from our side of the wall. It was related by one of our officers, a young Scotchman, who was a native of the place, and while I state that I give it to the best of my recollection, I could have wished, as the tale is a true one, that it had fallen into the hands of the late lamented author of Waverly, who would have done greater justice to its merits.

THE OFFICER'S STORY.

On the banks of the river Carron, near the celebrated village of that name, which shows its glowing fields of fiery furnaces, stirred by ten thousand imps of darkness, as if all the devils from the nether world there held perpetual revels, toasting their red hot irons and twisting them into all manner of fantastic shapes—tea-kettles, ten-pounders, and ten-penny nails—I say, that near that village—not in the upper and romantic region of it, where old Norval of yore fished up his basketful of young Norvals —but about a mile below where the river winds through the low country, in a bight of it there stands a stately two-story house, dashed with pale pink and having a tall chimney at each end, sticking up like a pair of asses' ears. The main building is supported by a brace of wings not large enough to fly away with it, but standing in about the same proportions that the elbows of an easy chair do to its back. The hall door is flanked on each side by a pillar of stone as thick as my leg, and over it there is a niche in the wall which in the days of its glory might have had the honour of lodging Neptune or Nicodemus, but is now devoted exclusively to the loves of the sparrows.

Viewed at a little distance the mansion still

wears a certain air of imposing gentility—looking like the substantial retreat of one who had
well feathered his nest upon the high seas, or
as an adventurer in foreign lands.   But a nearer
approach shews that the day of its glory has
long departed, the winds are howling through
the glassless casements, the roof is plastered
by the pigeons, the pigs and the poultry are
galloping at large over the ruins of the garden-
wall, luxuriating in its once costly shrubbery,
and a turkey is most likely seen at the hall-door,
staring the visitor impertinently in the face, and
blustering as if he would say, " if you want me
you must down with the dust."

Had that same turkey, however, lived some
six score years before, in the life-time, or in
the death-time of the last of its lairds, he
would have found himself compelled to gabble
to another tune, for in place of being allowed
to insult his guests in his master's hall, he would
have been called upon to share his merry-
thought for their amusement at the festive
board.

That the last laird of Abbots-Haugh had lived like a right good country gentleman all of the olden days, the manner of his death will testify, for though his living history is lost in the depth of time, his death is still alive in the recollections of our existing great grandfathers. He was, to the best of my belief, wifeless and relationless, nevertheless, when the time approached that "the old man he must die," he did as all prudent men do, made his temporal arrangements previous to the settling of that last debt which he owed to nature.

The laird, it appeared, was not haunted by the fears of most men, which forbid the inspection of their last testaments, until the last shovelful of earth has secured their remains from the wrath of disappointed expectants, and from a conscious dread too that the only tears that would otherwise be shed at their obsequies, would be by the undertaker and his assistants with their six big black horses; but the laird, as before said, was altogether another manner of man, and his last request was, that certain persons should consider themselves his executors, that they should open his will the moment the breath was out of his body, and that they should see his last injunctions faithfully executed as they hoped that he should rest calmly in his grave.

The laird quietly gave up the ghost, and his last wish was complied with ; when, to the no small astonishment of the executors, the only bequest which his will decreed was, that every man within a given distance of his residence was to be invited to the funeral, and that they were all to be filled blind drunk before the commencement of the procession !

This was certainly one of the most jovial wills that was ever made by a dying man, and it was acted upon to the letter.

The appointed day arrived, and so did the guests too; and although the invitations had only extended to the men, yet did their wives, like considerate folks as they always are, reflect that a dying man cannot have all his wits about him, and had any one but taken the trouble to remind him that there were such things as angels even in this world, they would no doubt have been included, and with that view of the case they considered it their duty to give their aid in the *mournful* ceremony.

The duties of the day at length began as was usual on those days, by—

" One-mile prayers and half-mile graces,"

to which the assembled multitude impatiently listened with their

" Toom wames and lang wry faces."

That ceremony over, they proceeded with all due diligence to honour the last request of the departed laird.

The droves of bullocks, sheep, and turkeys, which had been sacrificed for the occasion, were served up at mid-day, and as every description of foreign and British wines, spirits, and ales flowed in pailfuls, the executors indulged in the

G

very reasonable expectation that the whole party would be sufficiently glorious to authorize their proceeding with their last duty so as to have it over before dark : but they had grossly miscalculated the capacities of their guests, for even at dusk when they considered themselves compelled to put the procession in motion at all hazards, it was found that many of them were not more than " half seas over."

The distance from Abbots-Haugh to the dormitory of the parish-church is nearly two miles, the first half of the road runs still between two broad deep ditches which convey the drainings of these lowlands into the river ; the other half is now changed by the intersection of the great canal, but an avenue formed by two quick-set hedge-rows still marks its former line.

Doctor Mac Adam had not in those days begun to disturb the bowels of the harmless earth, by digging for stones wherewith to deface its surface, so that the roads were perfect evergreens, (when nobody travelled upon them,) but at the period I speak of, a series of wet weather and perpetual use had converted them into a sort of hodge-podge, which contributed nothing towards maintaining the gravity of the unsteady multitude now in motion, so that although the hearse started with some five or six hundred followers, all faithful and honest in their purpose to see the end of the ceremony, there were not above as many dozens who succeeded in following it into the church-yard, which it reached about midnight. These few however went on in the discharge of their duty and proceeded to remove the coffin from the hearse to its intended receptacle, but to their utter consternation there was no longer a coffin or a corpse there !

Tam O'Shanter lived a generation later than the period of my history, and I believe that there were few Scotchmen even in his days who were altogether free from supernatural dread however well primed with whiskey; but certain it is, that on this occasion every bonnet that was not on a bald head rose an inch or two higher, and many of them were pitched off altogether, as they began to reason (where reason there was none) as to the probable flight of the coffin; and though they were unanimously of opinion that it had gone the Lord knows where, yet they at last agreed that it was nevertheless a duty they owed the deceased to go back to Abbots-Haugh and inquire whether the laird had not returned. They accordingly provided themselves with lanterns, and examined all parts of the road on their way back, which was easily traced by the sleeping and besotted persons of the funeral party which formed a continuous link from the one place to the other—some lying in the road —some stuck fast in the hedges, but the majority three parts drowned in the ditches. When our return party arrived near the site of the present distillery, which happened to be the deepest part of the way, they heard something floundering at a frightful rate at the edge of a pool of water on the road side, and which, on examination, proved to be a huge old woman who was in the habit of supplying the farmers in that part of the country with loaf bread for their

Sunday's breakfasts; she was holding on fiercely
by what appeared to be the stump of a tree,
while her nether end was immersed in the water,
but when they went to pull her out, they found
to their delight and astonishment that she was
actually holding on by the end of the lost coffin,
which had fallen at the edge of the pool. Old
Nelly could give no information as to how it got
there, she had some recollection of having been
shoved into the hearse at first starting, but knew
nothing more until she found herself up to her
oxters in the water, holding fast by something
—that she had bawled until she was hoarse,
and had now nothing but a kick left to tell the
passers by that a poor creature was perishing.
She had most probably been reposing on the
coffin as a place of rest, and been jolted a step
beyond it when the two fell out.

A council was now called to determine the
proper mode of further proceeding, when it was
moved and carried that a vote of censure be
passed upon the executors for having failed to
fulfil the provisions of the laird's will, for in

place of being drunk, as they ought to have been, they were all shamefully sober; secondly, that it was in vain to repeat the attempt to bury him until the conditions upon which he died were complied with, for he had pledged himself not to rest quiet in his grave if it was neglected, and it was evident from what he had already done that he was not to be humbugged, but would again slip through their fingers unless justice was done to his memory, and it was therefore finally resolved that the laird be carried back to his own hall, there to lie in state until the terms of his testament were confirmed and ratified beyond dispute.

Back, therefore, they went to Abbots-Haugh, and set themselves again right honestly to work, as good and loyal vassals to obey their master's last behests, and that they at length succeeded in laying the restless spirit may be inferred from the fact that it was the afternoon of the third day from that time before the party felt themselves in a condition to renew the attempt to complete the ceremony; however it was then done effectually, as for fear of accidents, and not to lose sight of the coffin a second time, as many as there was room for took post on the top of it, provided with the means of finishing, at their destination, what the defunct might have considered underdone on their departure. And accordingly when they had at last succeeded in depositing the coffin within the family vault, and had set the bricklayers to work, they renewed their revels in the church-yard, until they finally saw the tomb closed over one of the most eccentric characters that ever went into it.

I shall now take leave of tales, and recommence the narration of passing events by mentioning that while we remained at Valle, one of our officers made an amusing attempt to get up a pack of hounds. He offered a dollar a head for anything in the shape of a dog that might be brought to him, which in a very short time furnished his kennel with about fifteen couple, composed of poodles, sheep-dogs, curs, and every species but the one that was wanted.

When their numbers became sufficiently formidable to justify the hope that there might be a few noses in the crowd gifted with the sense of smelling something more game than their porridge-pots; the essay was made, but they proved a most ungrateful pack, for they were no sooner at liberty than every one went howling away to his own home as if a tin kettle had been tied to his tail. (A prophetic sort of feeling of what would inevitably have befallen him had he remained a short time longer.)

Scotchmen are generally famed for the size of their noses, and I know not whether it is that on service they get too much crammed with snuff and gunpowder, or from what other cause, but certain it is that they do not prove themselves such useful appendages to the countenance there as they do in their own country, in scenting out whatever seemeth good unto the wearer, for I remember one day, while waging war against the snipes on the flooded banks of the Rio Maior, in passing by the rear of a large country house which was occupied by the commander-in-chief of the cavalry, (Sir Stapleton Cotton,) I was quite horrified to find myself all at once amidst the ruins of at least twenty dozen of sheep's heads, unskinned and unsinged, to the utter disgrace of about two thousand highland noses belonging to the forty-second and seventy-ninth regiments, which had, all the while of their accumulation, been lodged within a mile, and not over and above well provided with that national standing dish.

I will venture to say, that had such a deposit been made any evening on the North Inch of Perth in the days of their great grandfathers, there would have been an instinctive gathering of all the clans between the Tay and Cairngorum before day-light next morning.

CHAP. VII.

" Blood and destruction shall be so in use,
    And dreadful objects so familiar,
    That mothers shall but smile when they behold
    Their infants quartered with the hands of war."

THE month of March, eighteen hundred and
eleven, showed the successful workings of Lord
Wellington's admirable arrangements. The
hitherto victorious French army, which, under
their " spoilt child of fortune," had advanced to
certain conquest, were now obliged to bundle
up their traps and march back again, leaving
nearly half their numbers to fatten the land
which they had beggared. They had fallen,
too, on nameless ground, in sickness and in

want, and without a shot, by which their friends and relatives might otherwise have proudly pointed to the graves they filled.

Portugal, at that period, presented a picture of sadness and desolation which it is sickening to think of—its churches spoliated, its villages fired, and its towns depopulated.

It was no uncommon sight, on entering a cottage, to see in one apartment some individuals of the same family dying of want, some perishing under the brutal treatment of their oppressors, and some (preferring death to dishonour) lying butchered upon their own hearths.

These were scenes which no Briton could behold without raising his voice in thanksgiving to the Author of all good, that the home of his childhood had been preserved from such fearful visitations ; and yet how melancholy it is to reflect that even in that cherished home there should be many self-styled patriots, who not only grumble at, but would deny their country's pittance to those who devoted the best part of their lives, sacrificed their health, and cheerfully scattered their limbs in rolling the tide of battle from its door.

I lament it feelingly but not selfishly, for as far as I am individually concerned, my country and I are quits. I passed through the fiery ordeal of these bloody times and came out scatheless. While I parted from its service on the score of expediency, it is to me a source of pride to reflect (may I be pardoned the expression) that we parted with mutual regret. That she may never again require a re-union with such an humble individual as myself may heaven in its infinite mercy forfend; but if she does, I am happy in the feeling that I have still health and strength, and a heart and soul devoted to her cause.

Massena's retreat having again called the sword from its scabbard, where it had slumbered for months, it was long ere it had another opportunity of running to rust through idleness, seeing that it was not only in daily communication with the *heads* of the enemy's corps in the course of their return through Portugal, but wherever else these same heads were visible, and for a year and a half from that date they were rarely out of sight.

On the 9th, we came up with their rear-guard on a table land near Pombal. We had no force with which to make any serious attack upon it, so that it was a day's dragooning, " all cry and little wool." We had one company mixed among them from day-light until dark, but they came back to us without a scratch.

On the morning of the 11th, finding that the enemy had withdrawn from the scene of the former day's skirmish, we moved in pursuit towards the town, which they still occupied as an advanced post. Two of our companies, with some Caçadores and a squadron of the royal dragoons, made a dash into it, driving the enemy out, and along with a number of prisoners captured the baggage of young Soult.

I know not whether young Soult was the son of old Soult or only the son of his father; all I know is, that by the letters found in his portmanteau, he was the colonel of that name.

His baggage, I remember, was mounted on a
stately white horse with a Roman nose and a
rat tail, which last I believe is rather an unusual
appendage to a horse of that colour, but he was
a waggish looking fellow, and probably had
shaken all the hairs out of his tail in laughing
at the contents of the portmanteau of which he
was the bearer.

He and his load were brought to the hammer
the same day by his captors, and excited much
merriment among us. I wish that I felt myself
at liberty to publish an inventory of the contents
of a French officer's portmanteau, but as they
excited such excess of laughter in a horse I fear
it would prove fatal to my readers—not to men
tion (as I see written on some of the snug cor-
ners of our thoroughfares) that " decency forbids."
Suffice it that it abounded in luxuries which we
dreamt not of.

Next day, the 12th, in following the retiring
foe we came to the field of Redinha. I have
never in the course of my subsequent military
career seen a more splendid picture of war than

was there shewn. Ney commanded the opposing force, which was formed on the table land in front of the town in the most imposing shape. We light folks were employed in the early part of the action in clearing the opposing *lights* from the woods which flanked his position, and in the course of an hour about thirty thousand British, as if by magic, were seen advancing on the plain in three lines, with the order and precision of a field day: the French disappeared before them like snow under the influence of a summer's sun. The forces on both sides were handled by masters in the art.

A late lady writer (Miss Pardoe) I see has now peopled Redinha with banditti, and as far as my remembrance goes, they could not have selected a more favourable position, with this single but important professional drawback, that there can be but few folks thereabout worth robbing.

I know not what class of beings were its former tenants, but at the time I speak of, the

curse of the Mac Gregors was upon them, for
the retiring enemy had given

" Their roofs to the flames and their flesh to the eagles,"

and there seemed to be no one left to record its
history.

After the peace, in 1814, I met, at a ball in
Castel Sarrazin, the colonel who commanded the
regiment opposed to us in the wood on that
occasion.   He confessed that he had never been
so roughly handled, and had lost four hundred
of his men.   He was rather a rough sort of a
diamond himself, and seemed anxious to keep
his professional hand in practice, for he quarrel-
ed that same night with one of his countrymen
and was bled next morning with a small sword.

From Redinha we proceeded near to Condeixa,
and passed that day and night on the road side
in comparative peace.   Not so the next, for at
Casal Nova, on the 14th, we breakfasted, dined,
and supped on powder and ball.

Our general of division was on leave of

absence in England during this important period, and it was our curse in the interim to fall into the hands successively of two or three of the worthiest and best of men, but whose only claims to distinction as officers was their sheet of parchment. The consequence was, that whenever there was any thing of importance going on, we were invariably found leaving undone those things which we ought to have done, and doing that which we ought not to have done. On the occasion referred to we were the whole day battering our brains out against stone walls at a great sacrifice of life, whereas, had we waited with common prudence until the proper period, when the flank movements going on under the direction of our illustrious chief had begun to take effect, the whole of the loss would have been on the other side, but as it was, I am afraid that although we carried our point we were the greatest sufferers. Our battalion had to lament the loss of two very valuable officers on that occasion, Major Stewart and Lieutenant Strode.

At the commencement of the action, just as the mist of the morning began to clear away, a section of our company was thrown forward among the skirmishers, while the other three remained in reserve behind a gentle eminence, and the officer commanding it, seeing a piece of rising ground close to the left, which gave him some uneasiness, he desired me to take a man with me to the top of it, and to give him notice if the enemy attempted any movement on that side. We got to the top; but if we had not found a couple of good sized stones on the spot, which afforded shelter at the moment, we should never have got any where else, for I don't think they expended less than a thousand shots upon us in the course of a few minutes. My companion, John Rouse, a steady sturdy old rifleman, no sooner found himself snugly covered, than he lugged out his rifle to give them one in return, but the slightest exposure brought a dozen balls to the spot in an instant, and I was amused to see old Rouse, at every attempt, jerking back his head with a sort of knowing grin, as if it were only a parcel of schoolboys, on the other side, threatening him with snowballs; but seeing, at last, that his time for action was not yet come, he withdrew his rifle, and, knowing my inexperience in those matters, he very good-naturedly called to me not to expose myself looking out just then, for, said he, " there will be no moving among them while this shower continues."

When the shower ceased we found that they had also ceased to hold their formidable post, and, as quickly as may be, we were to be seen standing in their old shoes, mixed up with some of the forty-third, and among them the gallant Napier, the present historian of the Peninsular War, who there got a ball through his body which seemed to me to have reduced the remainder of his personal history to the compass of a simple paragraph: it nevertheless kept him but a very short while in the back-ground.

I may here remark that the members of that distinguished family were singularly unfortunate in that way, as they were rarely ever in any serious action in which one or all of them did not get hit.

The two brothers in our division were badly wounded on this occasion, and, if I remember right, they were also at Busaco; the naval captain, (the present admiral of that name,) was there as an amateur, and unfortunately caught it on a spot where he had the last wish to be distinguished, for, accustomed to face broadsides on his native element, he had no idea of taking in a ball in any other direction than from the front, but on shore we were obliged to take them just as they came!

This severe harassing action closed only with the day-light, and left the French army wedged in the formidable pass of Miranda de Corvo.

They seemed so well in hand that some doubt was entertained whether they did not intend to burst forth upon us; but, as the night closed in, the masses were seen to melt, and at day-light next morning they were invisible.

I had been on picquet that night in a burning village, and the first intimation we had of their departure was by three Portuguese boys, who had been in the service of French officers, and who took the opportunity of the enemy's night march to make their escape—they seemed well fed, well dressed, and got immediate employment in our camp, and they proved themselves very faithful to their new masters. One of them continued as a servant to an officer for many years after the peace.

In the course of the morning we passed the brigade of General Nightingale, composed of Highlanders, if I remember right, who had made a flank movement to get a slice at the enemy's rear guard; but he had arrived at the critical pass a little too late.

In the afternoon we closed up to the enemy at Foz d'Aronce, and, after passing an hour in feeling for their different posts, we began to squat ourselves down for the night on the top of a bleak hill, but soon found that we had other fish to fry. Lord Wellington, having a prime nose for smelling out an enemy's blunder, no sooner came up than he discovered that Ney had left himself on the wrong side of the river, and immediately poured down upon him with our division, Picton's, and Pack's Portuguese, and, after a sharp action, which did not cease until after dark, we drove him across the river with great loss.

I have often lamented in the course of the war that battalion officers, on occasions of that kind, were never entrusted with a peep behind the curtain. Had we been told before we advanced that there was but a single division in our front, with a river close behind them, we would have hunted them to death, and scarcely a man could have escaped; but, as it was, their greatest loss was occasioned by their own fears and precipitancy in taking to the river at unfordable places—for we were alike ignorant of the river, the localities, or the object of the attack; so that when we carried the position, and exerted ourselves like prudent officers to hold our men in hand, we were, from want of infor-

mation, defeating the very object which had
been intended, that of hunting them on to the
finale.

When there is no object in view beyond the
simple breaking of the heads of those opposed
to us, there requires no speechification ; but, on
all occasions, like the one related, it ought never
to be lost sight of—it is easily done—it never,
by any possibility, can prove disadvantageous,
and I have seen many instances in which the
advantages would have been incalculable. I
shall mention as one—that three days after the
battle of Vittoria, in following up the retreating
foe, we found ourselves in a wood, engaged in a
warm skirmish, which we concluded was occasioned by our pushing the enemy's rear guard
faster than they found it convenient to travel ;
but, by and bye, when they had disappeared,
we found that we were near the junction of two
roads, and that we had all the while been close
in, and engaged with the flank of another
French division, which was retiring by a road
running parallel with our own. The road (and

that there was a retiring force upon it) must,
or ought to have been known to some of our
staff officers, and had they only communicated
their information, there was nothing to have
prevented our dashing through their line of
march, and there is little doubt, too, but the
thousands which passed us, while we stood there
exchanging shots with them, would have fallen
into our hands.

The day after the action at Foz d'Aronce was
devoted to repose, of which we stood much in
want, for we had been marching and fighting
incessantly from day-light until dark for several
consecutive days, without being superabundantly
provisioned; and our jackets, which had been tolerably tight fits at starting, were now beginning
to sit as gracefully as sacks upon us. When
wounds were abundant, however, we did not
consider it a disadvantage to be low in flesh,
for the poorer the subject the better the patient!

A smooth ball or a well polished sword will
slip through one of your transparent gentlemen
so gently that he scarcely feels it, and the holes

close again of their own accord. But see the
smash it makes in one of your turtle or turkey
fed ones ! the hospital is ruined in finding materials to reduce his inflammations, and it is
ten to one if ever he comes to the scratch
again.

On descending to the river side next morning to
trace the effects of the preceding night's combat,
we were horrified and disgusted by the sight of
a group of at least five hundred donkeys standing there ham-strung. The poor creatures
looked us piteously in the face, as much as to
say, " Are you not ashamed to call yourselves
human beings ?" And truly we were ashamed
to think that even our enemy could be capable
of such refinement in cruelty. I fancy the truth
was, they were unable to get them over the
river, they had not time to put them to death,
and, at the same time, they were resolved that
we should not have the benefit of their services.
Be that as it may, so disgusted and savage were
our soldiers at the sight, that the poor donkeys
would have been amply revenged, had fate, at

that moment, placed five hundred Frenchmen in our hands, for I am confident that every one of them would have undergone the same operation.

The French having withdrawn from our front on the 16th, we crossed the Ciera, at dawn of day, on the 17th; the fords were still so deep, that, as an officer with an empty haversack on my back, it was as much as I could do to flounder across it without swimming. The soldiers ballasted with their knapsacks, and the sixty rounds of ball cartridge were of course in better fording trim. We halted that night in a grove of cork trees, about half a league short of the Alva.

Next morning we were again in motion, and found the enemy's rear-guard strongly posted on the opposite bank of that river.

The Alva was wide, deep, and rapid, and the French had destroyed the bridge of Murcella, and also the one near Pombeira. Nevertheless, we opened a thundering cannonade on those in our front, while Lord Wellington, having, with extraordinary perseverance, succeeded in throwing three of his divisions over it higher up, threatening their line of retreat—it obliged those opposed to us to retire precipitately, when our staff corps, with wonderful celerity, having contrived to throw a temporary bridge over the river, we passed in pursuit and followed until dark; we did not get another look at them that day, and bivouacked for the night in a grove of pines, on some swampy high lands, by the road side, without baggage, cloaks, or eatables of any kind.

Who has not passed down Blackfriars-road of an evening? and who has not seen, in the vicinity of Rowland Hill's chapel, at least half a dozen gentlemen presiding each over his highly polished tin case, surmounted by variegated lamps, and singing out that most enchanting of all earthly melodies to an empty stomach, that has got a sixpence in its clothly casement, " hot, all hot!" The whole concern is not above the size of a drum, and, in place of deal-

ing in its empty sounds, rejoices in mutton-
pies, beef-steaks, and kidney-puddings, " hot,
all hot !" If the gentlemen had but followed us
to the wars, how they would have been worshipped in such a night, even without their lamps.

In these days of invention, when every sug-
gestion for ameliorating the condition of the
soldier is thankfully received, I, as one, who
have suffered severely by outward thawings and
inward gnawings, beg to found my claim to the
gratitude of posterity, by proposing that, when
a regiment is ordered on active service, the
drummers shall deposit their sheep-skins and
their cat-o'-nine tails in the regimental store-
room, leaving one cat only in the keeping of the
drum major. And in lieu thereof that each
drummer be armed with a *tin drum* full of " hot,
all hot !" and that whenever the quarter-master
fails to find the *cold*, the odd cat in the keeping of the drum-major shall be called upon to
remind him of his duty.

If the simple utterance of the three magical

monosyllables already mentioned did not rally a
regiment more rapidly round the given point
than a tempest of drums and trumpets, I should
be astonished, and as we fought tolerably well
on empty stomachs, I should like to see what
we would not do on kidney puddings, " hot,
all hot!"

On the 19th we were again in motion at day-
light, and both on that day and the next, although we did not come into actual contact with
the enemy, we picked up a good many stragglers. We were obliged, however, to come to
a halt for several days from downright want, for
the country was a desert, and we had out-
marched our supplies. Until they came up,
therefore, we remained two days in one village,
and kept creeping slowly along the foot of the
Sierra, until our commissariat was sufficiently
re-inforced to enable us to make another dash.

I was amused at that time, in marching through
those towns and villages which had been the
head-quarters of the French army, to observe
the falling off in their respect to the Marquess

d'Alorna, a Portuguese nobleman, who had espoused their cause, and who, during Massena's advance, had been treated like a prince among them. On their retreat, however, it was easily seen that he was considered an incumbrance. Their names were always chalked on the doors of the houses they occupied, and we remarked that the one allotted to the unfortunate marquis grew gradually worse as we approached the frontier, and I remember that in the last village before we came to Celerico, containing about fifty houses, only a cow's share of the buildings had fallen to his lot.

We halted one day at Mello, and seeing a handsome-looking new church on the other side of the Mondego, I strolled over in the afternoon to look at it. It had all the appearance of having been magnificently adorned in the interior, but the French had left the usual traces of their barbarous and bloody visit. The doors were standing wide open, the valuable paintings destroyed, the statues thrown down, and mixed with them on the floor, lay the bodies of six or seven murdered Portuguese peasants. It was a cruel and a horrible sight, and yet in the midst thereof was I tempted to commit a most sacrilegious act, for round the neck of a prostrate marble female image, I saw a bone necklace of rare and curious workmanship, the only thing that seemed to have been saved from the general wreck, which I very coolly transferred to my pocket and in due time to my portmanteau. But a day of retribution was at hand, for both the portmanteau and the necklace went from me like a tale that is told, and I saw them no more.

It was the 28th before we again came in contact with the enemy at the village of Frexadas. Two companies of ours and some dragoons were detached to dislodge them, which they effected in gallant style, sending them off in confusion and taking a number of prisoners; but the advantage was dearly purchased by the death of our adjutant, Lieutenant Stewart. He imprudently rode into the main street of the village, followed by a few riflemen, before the French had had time to withdraw from it, and was shot from a window.

One would imagine that there is not much sense wrapped up in an ounce of lead, and yet it invariably selects our best and our bravest, (no great compliment to myself by the way, considering the quantity of those particles that must have passed within a yard of my body at different times, leaving all standing.) Its present victim was a public loss, for he was a shrewd, active, and intelligent officer; a gallant soldier, and a safe, jovial, and honourable companion.

I was not one of the party engaged on that occasion, but with many of my brother officers, watched their proceedings with my spy-glass from the church-yard of Alverca. Our rejoicings on the flight of the enemy were quickly turned into mourning by observing in the procession of our returning victorious party, the gallant adjutant's well-known bay horse with a dead body laid across the saddle. We at first indulged in the hope that he had given it to the use of some more humble comrade; but long ere they reached the village we became satisfied that the horse was the bearer of the inanimate remains of his unfortunate master, who but an hour before had left us in all the vigour of health, hope, and manhood. At dawn of day on the following morning the officers composing the advanced guard, dragoons, artillery, and riflemen, were seen voluntarily assembled in front of Sir Sidney Beckwith's quarters, and the body, placed in a wooden chest, was brought out and buried there amid the deep but silent grief of the spectators.

Brief, however, is the space which can be allotted to military lamentations in such times, for within a quarter of an hour we were again on the move in battle array, to seek laurels or death in another field.

Our movement that morning was upon Guarda, the highest standing town in Portugal, which is no joke, as they are rather exalted in their architectural notions—particularly in con-vent-building—and were even a thunder-charged cloud imprudent enough to hover for a week

within a league of their highest land, I verily
believe that it would get so saddled with monks,
nuns, and their accompanying iron bars, that it
would be ultimately unable to make its escape.

Our movement, as already said, was upon
Guarda, and how it happened, the Lord and
Wellington only knows, but even in that wild
mountainous region the whole British army
arriving from all points of the compass were
seen to assemble there at the same instant, and
the whole French army were to be seen at the
same time in rapid retreat within gun-shot
through the valley below us.

There must have been some screws loose
among our minor departments, otherwise such
a brilliant movement on the part of our chief
would not have gone for nothing. But notwithstanding that the enemy's masses were struggling
through a narrow defile for a considerable time,
and our cavalry and horse artillery were launch-
ed against them, three hundred prisoners were
the sole fruits of the day's work.

CHAP. VII.

The persecution of the guardian of two angels. A Caçadore and his mounted followers. A chief of hussars in his trousers. A chief of rifles in his glory, and a sub of ditto with two screws in the neck.

IN one of the first chapters of this book I not only pledged my constancy to my fair readers, but vowed to renew my addresses from time to time as opportunities offered. As my feet, however, have since trodden from one extremity of a kingdom to the other, and many months have, in the meanwhile, rolled away without giving me an opportunity of redeeming the pledge, I fear that my fidelity might be doubted if I delayed longer in assuring them that the spirit has all along been willing, but the subject fearfully wanting; for wherever I have wandered the angel of death has gone before, and carefully swept from the female countenance all lines of beauty, leaving nothing for the eye to dwell on but the hideous ruins of distress.

The only exceptions were our fellow travellers, for the country on our line of march, as already said, was reduced to a desert, and no one remained in it who had either wealth or strength to remove, and our regimental wife had deserted, but our gallant associates, the 43d and 52d regiments, had one each, who had embarked with them, and remained true to the brigade until the end of the war. One of them was remarkably pretty, and it did one's heart good to see the everlasting sweets that hung upon her lovely countenance, assuring us that our recollections of the past were not ideal, which they would otherwise have been apt to revolve themselves into from the utter disappearance of reality for so long a period.

The only addition to them which our division

could boast, were two smart substantial looking
Portuguese angels, who followed our two Caçadore regiments, and rode on mule-back under
the especial protection of their regimental chap-
lain. These two were a continual source of
amusement to us on the march whenever we
found ourselves at liberty to indulge in it. The
worthy father himself was quite a lady's man,
(Portuguese,) he was a short stout old fellow,
with a snuff-coloured coat buttoned up to the
throat, which was quite unnecessary with him,
seeing that he shaved and put on a clean shirt
sometimes as often as once a fortnight. The
round mealy-faced ball which he wore as a head
was surmounted by a tall cocked hat, and when
mounted on his bay pony in his Portuguese
saddle, which is boarded up like a bucket, (the
shape of his seat and thighs,) he was exactly
like some of the cuts I have seen of Hudibras
starting on his erratic expedition.

It was our daily amusement whenever we
could steal away from our regiment a short time,
for two or three of us to start with some design

against the Padré and his dark-eyed wards.
One of us would ride quietly up alongside of
him and another on that of the ladies as if we
wished to pass, but in wishing them the compliments of the season we of course contrived
to get ourselves entangled in conversation, while
a third officer of our party rode some distance
in the rear in readiness to take advantage of
circumstances.

The Padré was a good-natured old fellow,
fond of spinning a yarn, and as soon as one of
us had got him fairly embarked in his story, the
other began gradually to detach one or both of
the damsels from his side, according as the
inequalities of the road favoured the movement.
They entered into the frolic merrily, but still he
was so much alive that we rarely succeeded in
stealing one out of sight; but if we did by any
accident, it was a grand scene to see the scramble which he and his pony made after the fugitives, and on recovering the one, his rage on
his return to find that the other had also disappeared. After one of these successful expe-

ditions we found it prudent never to renew the attack until his wrath was assuaged, and it never abode with him long, so that week after week and year after year we continued to renew the experiment with various success.

It is amusing to think to what absurdities people will have recourse by way of amusement when subjects for it are scarce. It was long a favourite one with us to hunt a Caçadore as we called it. Their officers as well as our own were always mounted, and when their corps happened to be marching in our front, any officer who stopped behind, (which they frequently had occasion to do,) invariably, in returning to rejoin his regiment, passed ours at a full gallop; and on those occasions he had no sooner passed our first company than the officers of it were hard at his heels, the others following in succession as he cleared them, so that by the time he had reached the head of the regiment the whole of our officers had been in full chace. We never carried the joke too far, but made it a point of etiquette to stop short of our commanding officer, (who was not supposed to see what was going on,) and then fell quietly back to our respective places.

I have often seen the hunted devil look round in astonishment, but I do not think he ever saw the wit of the thing, and for that matter I don't know that my readers will feel that they are much wiser, but it was nevertheless amusing to us; and not without its use, for the soldiers enjoyed the joke, which, though trifling, helped to keep up that larking spirit among them, which contributed so much towards the superiority and the glory of our arms. In times of hardship and privation the officer cannot be too much alive to the seizing of every opportunity, no matter how ridiculous, if it serves to beguile the soldier of his cares.

On the 1st of April we again closed up with the enemy on the banks of the Coa, near Sabugal. It was a wet muggy afternoon near dusk when we arrived at our ground, and I was sent, with the company which I had charge of, on picquet to cover the left front of our position.

The enemy held an opposite post on our side of the river, and I was ordered if they were civil to me not to interfere with them, but in the event of the reverse, to turn them over to their own side. My stomach was more bent upon eating than fighting that evening, and I was glad to find that they proved to be *gentlemen*, and allowed me to post my sentries as close as I pleased without interruption.

I found one of our German hussar videttes on a rising ground near me, and received an order from my brigadier to keep him there until he was relieved, and I accordingly placed a rifleman alongside of him for his better security, but after keeping him an hour or two in the dark and no relief appearing, I was forced to let him go or to share my slender allowance with him, for the poor fellow (as well as his horse) was starving. I have seen the day, however, that I would rather have dispensed with my dinner (however sharp set) than the services of one of those thorough-bred soldiers, for they were as singularly intelligent and useful on out-

post duty, as they were effective and daring in
the field.

The first regiment of hussars were associated
with our division throughout the war and were
deserved favourites. In starting from a swampy
couch and bowling along the road long ere dawn
of day, it was one of the romances of a soldier's life to hear them chanting their national
war songs—some three or four voices leading
and the whole squadron joining in the chorus.
As I have already said, they were no less daring
in the field than they were surpassingly good on
out-post duty. The hussar was at all times
identified with his horse, he shared his bed and
his board, and their movements were always
regulated by the importance of their mission. If we saw a British dragoon at any time
approaching in full speed, it excited no great
curiosity among us, but whenever we saw one
of the first hussars coming on at a gallop it was
high time to gird on our swords and bundle up.

Their chief, too, was a perfect soldier, and
worthy of being the leader of such a band, for

he was to them what the gallant Beckwith was to us—a father, as well as a leader.

He was one who never could be caught napping. They tell a good anecdote of him after the battle of Toulouse, when the news arrived of the capture of Paris and Bonaparte's abdication. A staff officer was sent to his outpost quarter to apprise him of the cessation of hostilities—it was late when the officer arrived, and after hearing the news, the colonel proceeded to turn into bed as usual, " all standing," when the officer remarked with some surprise, " Why, colonel, you surely don't mean to sleep in your clothes to-night, when you know there is an armistice ?"

" Air mistress or no air mistress," replied the veteran, " by Got I sleeps in my breeches !"

We remained another day in front of Sabugal, and as it was known that Reynier held that post with his single corps unsupported, Lord Wellington resolved to punish him for his temerity.

The day dawned on the morning of the 3d

of April, however, rather inauspiciously. Aurora did not throw off her night-cap at the usual hour, and when she could no longer delay the ceremony she shed such an abundance of dewy tears that Sabugal, with its steel-clad heights, remained invisible to the naked eye at the distance of a few hundred yards, which interfered materially with that punctuality in the combined movements so necessary to ensure the complete success of our enterprize. Leaving, therefore, to those concerned to account for their delays, my object in renewing this battle is to pay a last tribute to the memory of Sir Sidney Beckwith, the hero of that day.

He, as he had been directed, moved his brigade to a ford of the Coa, and was there waiting further orders, when a staff officer rode up, and hastily demanded why he had not attacked ?

Beckwith was an actor of the immortal Nelson's principle—that if a commander is in doubt he never can do wrong in placing himself alongside of the enemy. We instantly uncorked our muzzle-stoppers, off with our lock-caps, and our four companies of riflemen, led through the river, (which was deep and rapid,) followed by the 43d, driving in the enemy's picquet which defended it. The officer commanding, left his sky-blue cloak fluttering in the breeze on the top of a furze bush, and I felt a monstrous inclination to transfer it to my own shoulders, for it was an article of which I happened, at that moment, to be in especial want; but as it was the beginning of a battle in place of the end of one, and I had an insurmountable objection to fight under false colours, I passed it by.

As soon as we gained the summit of the hill it became as clear as the mist that we were regularly in for it. Beckwith, finding himself alone and unsupported, in close action, with only hundreds to oppose to the enemy's thousands, at once saw and felt all the danger of his situation; but he was just the man to grapple with any odds, being in his single person a host —of a tall commanding figure and noble countenance, with a soul equal to his appearance—

he was as Napier says, " a man equal to rally an army in flight."

Our four companies had led up in skirmishing order, driving in the enemy's light troops ; but the summit was defended by a strong compact body, against which we could make no head ; but opening out, and allowing the 43d to advance, they, with a tearing volley and a charge, sent the enemy rolling into the valley below, when the rifles again went to work in front, sticking to them like leeches.

The hill we had just gained became our rally-post for the remainder of the day, and, notwithstanding the odds on the side of the enemy, they were never able to wrest it from us. Our force was as well handled as theirs was badly, so that in the successive and desperate encounters which took place, both in advance and in retreat, we were as often to be seen in their position as they were in ours.

Beckwith himself was the life and soul of the fray; he had been the successful leader of those

who were then around him in many a bloody
field, and his calm, clear, commanding voice
was distinctly heard amid the roar of battle, and
cheerfully obeyed. He had but single companies to oppose to the enemy's battalions;
but, strange as it may appear, I saw him twice
lead successful charges with but two companies
of the 43d, against an advancing mass of the
enemy. His front, it is true, was equal to
theirs, and such was his daring, and such
the confidence which these hardy soldiers had
in him, that they went as fiercely to work
single-handed as if the whole army had been
at their heels.

Beckwith's manner of command on those occasions was nothing more than a familiar sort of
conversation with the soldier. To give an idea
of it I may as well mention that in the last
charge I saw him make with two companies of
the 43d, he found himself at once opposed to a
fresh column in front, and others advancing on
both flanks, and, seeing the necessity for immediate retreat, he called out, " Now, my lads,

we'll just go back a little if you please." On
hearing which every man began to run, when
he shouted again, " No, no, I don't mean that
—we are in no hurry—we'll just walk quietly
back, and you can give them a shot as you go
along." This was quite enough, and was obeyed
to the letter—the retiring force keeping up a
destructive fire, and regulating their movements
by his, as he rode quietly back in the midst of
them, conversing aloud in a cheerful encouraging
manner—his eye all the while intently watching
the enemy to take advantage of circumstances.
A musket-ball had, in the meantime, shaved his
forehead, and the blood was streaming down his
countenance, which added not a little to the
exciting interest of his appearance. As soon as
we had got a little way up the face of our hill,
he called out, " Now, my men, this will do—
let us shew them our teeth again!" This was
obeyed as steadily as if the words halt, front,
had been given on parade, and our line was instantly in battle array, while Beckwith, shaking
his fist in the faces of the advancing foe, called

out to them, " Now, you rascals, come on here if you dare !" Those he addressed shewed no want of courage, but, for a while, came boldly on to the tune of *old trousers,** notwithstanding the fearful havoc we were making in their ranks; but they could not screw themselves up the long disputed hill—the 52d (two battalions) had, by this time, come into the line of battle, and were plying them hard on the right, while our rifles were peppering them on their front and left, and, as soon as they came near enough, another dash by Beckwith, at the head of the 43d, gave them the *coup de grace.* The fate of the day was now decided—the net which had been wove

* *Old trousers* was a name given by our soldiers to the point of war which is beat by the French drummers in advancing to the charge. I have, when skirmishing in a wood, and a French regiment coming up to the relief of the opposing skirmishers, often heard the drum long before we saw them, and, on those occasions, our riflemen immediately began calling to each other, from behind the different bushes, " Holloa there ! look sharp ! for damn me, but here comes old trousers !"

in the morning, and which the state of the weather had prevented being brought to a crisis as
soon as was intended, now began to tighten
around them—the 5th division crossed by the
bridge of Sabugal, and the 3d, (I believe,) by
a ford to the right—and Reynier, seeing no
hopes of salvation but by immediate flight, very
speedily betook himself to it, and, I believe,
saved all that did not fall on the field of battle—
a piece of good fortune of which his conduct
that day shewed him undeserving, for, had not
the extraordinary state of the weather caused
the delays and mistakes which took place on our
side, he could scarcely have taken a man out of
the field.

While standing in our last position, awaiting
the attack in our front, I was much amused in
observing, on the opposite height, the approach
of our 3d division, unnoticed by the enemy—a
French column occupied the top of what seemed
to be almost a precipice overlooking the river;
but I observed some of the 60th riflés clamber-
ing up the face of it on all fours, and, to see

their astonishment, when they poked their heads over the brink, to find themselves within a couple of yards of a French column! They, of course, immediately concealed themselves under the bank; but it was curious to observe that they were unseen by the enemy, who were imprudent enough either to consider themselves secure on that side, or to give all their attention to the fight going on between their comrades and us; but certain it is they allowed the riflemen to gather there in formidable numbers. As we advanced immediately, the intervening rising ground prevented my seeing what took place, but on crowning the opposite height, which the French had just evacuated, we found, by the bodies on the ground, that they had just received a volley from a part of the third division—and one of the most deadly which had been fired that day.

Our cavalry had been astray during the fight, but they afterwards made two or three ineffectual attempts to break in upon the enemy's line of retreat.

Immediately after the action, we drew up behind an old cow-shed, which Lord Wellington occupied for a short time, while it poured torrents of rain. Sir William Erskine, with some of his horsemen, joined us there, and I heard him say to the commander-in-chief that he claimed no merit for the victory, as it belonged alone to Sidney Beckwith! I believe his lordship wanted no conjurer to tell him so, and did ample justice to the combatants, by stating in his dispatch that " this was one of the most glorious actions that British troops were ever engaged in."

To those accustomed to the vicissitudes of warfare it is no less curious to remark the many miraculous escapes from wounds than the recovery from them. As an instance of the former, I may observe, that, in the course of the action just related, I was addressing a passing remark to an officer near me, who, in turning round to answer, raised his right foot, and I observed a grape shot tear up the print which it had but that instant left in the mud. As an instance of the latter I shall here relate, (though rather misplaced,) that, at the storming of Badajos, in April, 1812, one of our officers got a musketball in the right ear, which came out at the back of the neck, and, though after a painful illness, he recovered, yet his head got a twist, and he was compelled to wear it, looking over the right shoulder. At the battle of Waterloo, in 1815, (having been upwards of three years with his neck awry,) he received a shot in the left ear, which came out within half an inch of his former wound in the back of the neck, and it set his head straight again!

This is an anecdote which I should scarcely have dared to relate were it not that, independent of my personal knowledge of the facts, the hero of it still lives to speak for himself, residing on his property, in Nottinghamshire, alike honoured and respected as a civilian, as he was loved and esteemed as a gentleman and a gallant soldier.*

After the action at Sabugal our brigade was

* Lieutenant Worsley.

placed under cover in the town, and a wild night it proved—the lightning flashed—the winds howled—and the rains rained. The house occupied by my brother sub and myself was a two-story one, and floored after the manner of some of our modern piers, with the boards six inches apart, and transferrable, if necessary, to a wider range, without the trouble of extracting or unscrewing nails.

The upper floor, as the most honoured portion, was assigned to us, while the first was reserved for the accommodation of some ten or a dozen well-starved inmates.

We had scarcely proceeded to dry our clothes, and to masticate the few remaining crumbs of biscuit, when we received a deputation from the lower regions, craving permission to join the mess; but, excepting the scrapings of our haversacks, we had literally nothing for ourselves, and were forced to turn a deaf ear to their entreaties, for there was no making them believe we were as destitute as we seemed. It was one of those cruel scenes to which the seats of war alone can furnish parallels, for their wan and wasted countenances shewed that they were wildly in want.

The following day saw Portugal cleared of its invaders, and the British standard once more unfurled within the Spanish boundary.

The French army retired behind the Agueda, and our division took possession of a portion of its former quarters, Fuentes d'Onoro, Gallegos, and Espeja. There we enjoyed a few days repose, of which we stood in much need, it having been exactly a month since we broke up in front of Santarem, and, as the foregoing pages shew, it was not spent in idleness.

CHAP. VIII.

National Characters.   Adventures of a pair of leather
Breeches.   Ditto of a pound of Beef.   Shewing what the
French General did not do, and a Prayer which he did
not pray ; with a few random Shots.

FUENTES, which was our first resting place,
was a very handsome village, and every family
so well known to the light division, that no
matter into which quarter the billet fell, the individual was received as an old and approved
friend.

The change from Portugal into Spain, as alluded to in my first work, was very striking.
In the former the monkish cowl seemed even
on ordinary occasions to be drawn over the face
of nature ; for though their sun was a heavenly

one, it shone over a dark and bigotted race ; and though they were as ripe for mischief as those of more enlightened nations, yet even in that they were woefully defective, and their joys seemed often sadly miscalled. But at the time I speak of, as if to shroud every thing in unfathomable gloom, the ravages of the enemy had turned thousands of what (to them) were happy homes, into as many hells—their domestic peace ruined—their houses and furniture fired, and every countenance bearing the picture of melancholy and wan despair.

Their damsels' cheeks wore no roses, yet did they wear soil enough on which to rear them. But at the same time be it remarked that I quarrel not with the countenance but with the soil, for I am a pale lover myself.

In Spain, on the contrary, health and joy seemed to beam on every countenance, and comfort in every dwelling. I have observed some writers quarrel with my former statement on this subject, and maintain that though the difference in appearance was remarkable, that so far as regards the article of cleanliness, the facts were not so. With these, however, I must still differ after giving every thing due consideration. The Portuguese did not assume to be a cleanly race, and they were a filthy one in reality. The Spaniards did affect to be the former, and I do think that they approached it as nearly as may be. I allude to the peasantry, for the upper and middling classes sink into immeasurable contempt in the comparison, but their peasantry I still maintain are as fine and as cleanly a class as I ever saw. Their dress is remarkably handsome, and though I can give no opinion as to the weekly value of soap expended on their manly countenances, yet in regard to the shirt, which is their greatest pride, and neatly embroidered in the bosom according to the position of the wearer in the minds of those on whom that portion of the ornamental devolves, I can vouch for their having shewn a clean one as often as need be. And though I do not feel myself at liberty to enter into the details of the dress of their lovely black-eyed damsels, I may be permitted to say that it is highly becoming to them; and, in short, I should have some dread of staking our national credit by parading the inmates of any chance village of our own against a similar one of theirs.

Their houses too are remarkably neat and cleanly, and would be comfortable were it not for those indefatigable villainous insects that play at a perpetual hop, skip, and jump, giving occasional pinches to the exposed parts of the inmate; and yet what warm country is exempt from them or something worse. Go into boasted America, and so great is the liberty of all classes there, that what with the hum of the musquitto above, and the bug below the blanket, the unfortunate wight, as I can testify, is regularly *hum-bugged* out of his natural repose. As I have taken a trip across the Atlantic for the foregoing example, I cannot resist giving an anecdote to shew that our brethren on that side of the water sometimes have a night's rest sacrificed to *inexpressible* causes as well as natural ones.

A gentleman at the head of the law there, (not the hangman,) told me that in his early days while the roads were yet in their infancy, he was in the habit of going his circuit on horseback, with nothing but a change of linen tacked to his crupper—that one day he had been overtaken by a shower of rain before he could reach the lonely cottage, which he had destined for his night's repose—and that it interfered materially with the harmony which had hitherto existed between him and his leather breeches, for he felt uncomfortable in them, and he felt uncomfortable out of them, arising from the dread that he might never be able to get into them again. His landlady, however, succeeded in allaying his fears for the moment, and having lent him one of her nether garments for present use, she finally consigned him to bed, with injunctions to sleep undisturbed, for that she would take especial care, while they underwent the necessary fiery ordeal, that she would put that within which should preserve their capacities undiminished.

Notwithstanding the satisfactory assurance on the part of the dame, a doubt continued still to hang on the mind of the man in the petticoat; and as " the mind disturbed denies the body rest," so was every attempt of his to close an eye, met by the vision of a pair of shrivelled leathers, until at length in a fit of feverish excitement he started from his couch determined to know the worst; and throwing open the door of the kitchen, he, to his no small astonishment, beheld his leathers not only filled, but well filled too, by the landlady herself, who there stood in them, toasting and turning round and round; neither so gracefully nor so fast as Taglioni, perhaps, but still she kept turning all the same; and it, most probably, was the smoke arising from the lawyer's wet leathers which Tom Moore saw curling so gracefully above the green elms when he wrote the Woodpecker.

But to return to the Peninsula. While it must be admitted that the hidalgo's evil is the lesser, I could, nevertheless, wish that the good old Spaniard would march a little more with the spirit of the times, for by the ordinary use of a small-tooth comb, he might be enabled to limit his *hair* hunting to the sports of the field.

The day after our arrival at Fuentes I was amused to hear one of our soldiers describing to a comrade his last night's fare in the new quarter. Soon after his taking possession of it, three days' rations had been served out to him, and his landlady, after reconnoitring it for a while with a wistful eye, at length proposed that they should mess together while he remained in their house, to which he readily assented; and by way of making a fair beginning, he cut off about a pound of the beef which he handed over to her, but at the same time allowing her about as much play with it as a cat does to a mouse—a precaution which he had reason to rejoice in, for he presently found it transferred to a kettle then boiling on the fire, containing, as he said, thirteen buckets of water, in which his pound of beef was floating about like a cork in the middle of the ocean! "Hilloah, my nice woman, says I, if you and I are to mess together I'll just trouble you to take out twelve buckets and a half of that water, and in place thereof, that you will be pleased to put in a pound of beef for every mouth which you intend shall keep mine in company — and if you choose to give some butter or a slice or two of bacon in addition, I shall not object to it, but I'll have none of your gammon!" The dispute ended in the rifleman's being obliged to fish out his pound of beef and keep it under his own protection.

Our repose in Fuentes was short. The garrison of Almeida was blockaded with a fortnight's provision only, and two companies of ours under Colonel Cameron were immediately dispatched to shoot their bullocks while grazing on the ramparts, which still further contracted their means of subsistence.

Lord Wellington had in the mean time hurried off to the south in consequence of the pressing importance of the operations of the corps under Marshal Beresford, leaving the main army for the time being under the command of Sir Brent Spencer. In the afternoon of the 16th of April we were hastily ordered under arms, and passing through Gallegos we were halted behind a hill on the banks of the Agueda, when we found that the movement had been occasioned by the passing of a convoy of provisions which the enemy were attempting to throw into Ciudad Rodrigo, and which was at that moment with its escort of two hundred men shut up in some inclosures of stone walls within half a mile of us surrounded by our dragoons.

I don't know how it happened, but we were kept there inactive for a couple of hours with eight thousand men sending in summonses for them to surrender, when a couple of our idle guns would have sent the loose wall about their ears and made them but too happy to be allowed to do so. But as it was, the garrison of Ciudad Rodrigo came out and carried them off triumphantly from under our noses.

" There's nae luck about the house,
    There's nae luck ava;
  There's nae luck about the house,
    When our gude man's awa."

This was the most critical period of the whole war; the destinies not only of England but of Europe hung upon it, and all hinged on the shoulders of one man,—that man was Wellington! I believe there were few even of those who served under him capable of knowing, still less of appreciating, the nature of the master-mind which there, with God's assistance, ruled all things; for he was not only the head of the army but obliged to descend to the responsibility of every department in it. In the different branches of their various duties, he received the officers in charge, as ignorant as schoolboys, and, by his energy and unwearied perseverance, he made them what they became—the most renowned army that Europe ever saw. Wherever he went at its head, glory followed its steps —wherever he was not—I will not say disgrace, but something near akin to it ensued, for it is

singular enough to remark that of all the distinguished generals who held separate commands in that army throughout the war Lord
Hill alone (besides the commander-in-chief)
came out of it with his fame untarnished by any
palpable error. In all his battles Lord Wellington appeared to us never to leave any thing to
chance. However desperate the undertaking—
whether suffering under momentary defeat, or
imprudently hurried on by partial success—we
ever felt confident that a redeeming power was
at hand, nor were we ever deceived. Those
only, too, who have served under such a master-
mind and one of inferior calibre can appreciate
the difference in a physical as well as a moral
point of view—for when in the presence of the
enemy, under him, we were never deprived of
our personal comforts until prudence rendered
it necessary, and they were always restored to
us again at the earliest possible moment. Under
the temporary command of others we have been
deprived of our baggage for weeks through the
timidity of our chief, and without the shadow

of necessity; and it is astonishing in what a degree the vacillation and want of confidence in a commander descends into the different ranks.

Of all the commanders in that army at the period I speak of, none stood more distinguished than he who was for the moment our head (the gallant Spencer,) and yet, singularly enough, the moment he was left to himself, not only his usual daring but all spirit of enterprise seemed to have forsaken him. Witness the escape of the French detachment as just related, as well as the various subsequent movements under him; whereas, within a few days, when in the field of Fuentes under Wellington, he was himself again.

While halted behind the hill already mentioned, I got my first look at the celebrated Guerilla chief, Don Julian Sanchez. He was a middling-sized thick-set fellow, with a Spanish complexion, well whiskered and mustached, with glossy black hair, and dressed in a hussar uniform. The peasantry of that part of the country used to tell rather a romantic story of the

cause which induced him to take up arms,—
namely, that the French had maltreated and
afterwards murdered his wife and family before
his face, besides firing his house, (cause enough
in all conscience,) and for which he amply
revenged himself, for he became the most celebrated throat-cutter in that part of the world.
His band when he first took the field did not
exceed fifty men, but about the period I speak
of his ranks had swelled to about fifteen hundred. They were a contemptible force in the field,
but brave, enterprising, and useful in their mountain fastnesses—in cutting off supplies and small
detachments. I did not see his troops until some
time after, when his heavy dragoons one day
crossed our line of march. They afterwards
cut a more respectable figure; but at that
period they looked a regular set of ragamuffins,
wearing cocked hats with broad white lace
round the edges; yellow coats, with many more
than button-holes, and red facings; breeches
of various colours and no stockings, but a sort
of shoe on the foot with a spur attached, and

their arms were as various as their colours; some with lances, some with carabines, and in short, every one seemed as if he had equipped himself in whatever the fortune of war had thrown in his way.

As the battle of Fuentes approached, our life became one of perpetual motion, and when I raised my head from its stone pillow in the morning, it was a subject of speculation to guess within a league of its next resting place, although we were revolving within a very limited space. Nothing clings so tenaciously to my mind as the remembrance of the different spots on which I have passed a night. Out of six years campaigning it is probable that I slept at least half the period under the open canopy of heaven, (barring latterly a sheet of canvas,) and though more than twenty years have since rolled over my head, I think I could still point out my every résting place.

On the night of the 1st of May I was sent from Alameda with thirty riflemen and six dragoons to watch a ford of the Agueda. The French held a post on the opposite side—but at daylight in the morning I found they had disappeared. Seeing a Spanish peasant descending on the opposite bank—and the river not being fordable to a person on foot, while its continuous roaring through its rugged course drowned every other voice—I detached one of the dragoons, who brought him over behind him, and as he told me that the French were, at that moment, on the move to the left, I immediately transmitted the information to head quarters. I was soon after ordered to join my battalion, which I found lodged in a stubble field about half way between Gallegos and Alameda, on a piece of rising ground which we had christened Kraüchenberg's hill, in compliment to that gallant captain of German hussars, who, with his single troop, had made a brilliant and successful charge from it the year before on the enemy's advancing horsemen.

The following night we had gone to bed in

the village of Espeja, but were called to arms in the middle of it, and took post in the wood behind.

With the enemy close upon us, our position was any thing but a safe one; but, as it included a conical hill, which commanded a view of their advance, Lord Wellington was anxious to retain it until the last possible moment.

The chief of the German hussars, who covered the reconnoitring party, looked rather blank when he found, next morning, that the infantry were in the act of withdrawing, and tried hard to persuade Beckwith to leave two companies of riflemen as a support, assuring him that all the cavalry in the world were unable to harm them in such a cover; but as the cover was, in reality, but a sprinkling of the Spanish oaks, our chief found it prudent to lend his deaf ear to the request. However, we all eventually reached the position of Fuentes unmolested— a piece of good luck which we had no right to expect, considering the military character of

our adversaries, and the nature of the ground
we had to pass over.

Having been one of the combatants in that
celebrated field, and having already given a history of the battle such as the fates decreed, it
only remains with me, following the example of
other historians, to *favour* the public with my
observations thereon.

In the course of my professional career several
events have occurred to bother my subaltern
notions on the principles of the art of war, and
none more than the battle of Fuentes; but to
convey a just idea of what I mean to advance,
it is necessary that I should describe the ground,
and while those who choose, may imagine that
they see it sketched by one who never before
drew any thing but the cork out of a bottle, or
a month's pay out of the hands of the paymaster, others, whose imaginations are not so
lively, must be contented in supposing themselves standing, with an army of thirty thousand men, between the streams of the Tourones

and Dos Casas, with our right resting on Nava
d'Aver, and our left on Fort Conception, a position extending seven miles.

The French advanced from Rodrigo with
forty-five thousand men to relieve their garrison,
which we had shut up in Almeida, which is in
rear of our left—and in place of going the
straight road to it, through Alameda and Fort
Conception, Massena spreads his army along
our whole front, and finally attacks the most
distant part of it, (Nava d'Aver.)

That, I believe, was all strictly according to
rule, for the purpose of preserving his base of
operations ; but I am labouring to shew that it
was an occasion on which Massena might and
ought to have set every rule at defiance, for, in
possession of a strong fortress under his own lee,
and another under that of his adversary, with an
army in the field exceeding ours by a fourth, he
ought to have known that no possible cast of the
dice could have enabled us to do more than maintain the blockade—that, if we gave him a defeat
it was impossible for us to follow it up, and if he

K

defeated us our ruin was almost inevitable—
in short, had I been Prince of Essling, I would
have thrust every thing but my fighting men
under the protection of the guns of Rodrigo,
and left myself, free and unfettered, to go where
I liked, do what I could, and, if need be, to
change bases with my adversary; and it is odd
to me if I would not have cut such capers as
would have astonished the great Duke himself.

From Fuentes to Alameda, a distance of between two and three miles, trusting to the rug-
gedness of the banks of the Dos Casos, the
position was nearly altogether unoccupied on
our side, and had Massena but taken the trouble
to wade through that stream as often as I had,
sometimes for love and sometimes for duty, he
would have found that it was passable in fifty
places—and, as the ground permitted it, had he
assembled twenty thousand infantry there, to be
thrust over at day-light, and held the rest of
his army in readiness to pounce upon the wing to
be attacked—and, had he prayed too, as did the
Scottish knight of old, (who had more faith in

his good sword than in the justice of his cause,) in these words, " O, Lord, we all know that the race is not to the swift nor the battle to the strong, and that, whichever side you take, will be sure to win; but, if you will, for this once, stand aside, and leave us two to fight it out, I shall be for ever obliged to you"— he might then have commenced the day's work with a tolerable prospect of success—for, if half the twenty thousand men, on reaching the top of the hill, remained to keep the one wing in check, and the remainder turned against the flank of the devoted one, while his main army took it in front, they would have had good cause to feel ashamed of themselves if they did not dispose of it long before human aid could have reached, and odd would it have been if the others had not then considered it high time to be off.

What alterations Lord Wellington would have made in his dispositions had he found himself opposed to one who held such fighting views as I do, it is not for me to say; but it is evident that

he estimated Massena at his full value when he
persisted in holding such an extended position
with an inferior army, while the other, with his
superior force, was satisfied with battering a portion of his best regimental* brains out against
the stone walls about Fuentes, and retiring,
at last, without attaining the object of his advance.

The foregoing reflections will, no doubt, to
many, appear wild ; but, with a tolerable knowledge of the ground, and of the comparative
strength, I am not the less satisfied that my plan
may be often tried with success.

In speaking of distance, however, it must not
be forgotten that in war the opposing bodies come
together with wonderful celerity; for, although

---

* The most formidable attack there on the 5th was made
by his most choice troops, and they succeeded in penetrating
to the high ground behind the church, where they were met
by a brigade of the 3d division, and routed with great
slaughter. One of the wounded prisoners pointed out to me
the body of a captain of grenadiers, (whose name I forget,)
who was renowned in their army for his daring.

soldiers do not see so far as severed lovers, who, by transmitting their looks at each other through the moon or some favoured star, contrive to kill space more quickly, yet the soldier, who has no great stomach for the battle, and sees his enemy in the morning almost out of sight, begins to reckon himself secure for that day, must be rather astonished when he finds how soon a cannon-ball makes up the difference between them!

Packenham, (the gallant Sir Edward,) who was then adjutant-general, led the brigade of the third division, which restored the battle in the village. He came to us immediately after, faint with excitement, where we were standing in reserve, and asked if any officer could oblige him with some wine or brandy—a calabash was unslung for his use, and after taking a small sip out of it, and eulogizing, in the handsomest manner, the conduct of the troops, he left us to renew his exertions wherever they might be wanted. He was as gallant a spirit as ever went into a field!

Lord Wellington, in those days, (as he was aware,) was always designated among the soldiers by the name of *Old Douro*. The morning after the battle, the celebrated D. M. of the guards, rode up to a group of staff officers, and demanded if any of them had seen Beau Douro this morning? His Lordship, who was there reclining on the ground in his boat cloak, started up, and said, " Well! by —— I never knew I was a beau before !" The same morning that officer came galloping to us with an order—our chief, (Sidney Beckwith,) who was never on horse-back except when his duty required it, had the greatest horror of the approach of a staff officer, who generally came at full speed until within a yard or two—seeing M. coming on as usual on his fiery dark chesnut, he began waving his hand for him to stop before he had got within fifty yards, and calling out, " Aye, aye, that will do ! we'll hear all you have got to say quite well enough !"

Among the many great and goodly names of general officers which the Army-list furnished, it was lamentable to see that some were sent from England, to commands in that army, who were little better than old wives,* and who would have been infinitely more at home in feeding the pigs and the poultry of a farm-yard than in furnishing food for powder in the field; yet so it was :—the neglect of such an one to deliver an order with which he had been entrusted, lost us the fame and the fruits of our victory, it prevented a gallant regiment from occupying the important post intended for it, and it cost that regiment its gallant chief, whose nice sense of honour could see no way of removing the stain which the neglect of his superior had cast upon his reputation, than by placing a pistol to his own head. His fate was sadly and deeply deplored by the whole army.

As this particular period furnished few occurrences to vary the monotony of the hammer-and-tongs sort of life we led, I shall take advantage

* No allusion to the last-mentioned officer, who was one of another stamp.

of the opportunity it affords to fire a few random
shots for the amusement of my readers.

SHOT THE FIRST.

The Duel.

On reaching Paris, after the battle of Waterloo, we found Johnny Petit in very bad humour;
and that three out of every four of the officers
in each army were not disposed of by private
contract, with pistols and small swords, must be
ascribed to our ignorance alike of their language
and their national method of conveying offence;
for, in regard to the first, although we were
aware that the *sacre bœuftake* and *sacre pomme
de terre,* with which we were constantly saluted,
were not applied complimentarily, yet, as the
connecting offensive links were lost to most of
us, these words alone were not looked upon as
of a nature requiring *satisfaction;* and, with

regard to practical insults, a favourite one of theirs, as we afterwards discovered, was to tread, as if by accident, on the toe of the person to be insulted. Now, as the natural impulse of the Englishman, on having his toe trodden on, is to make a sort of apology to the person who did it, by way of relieving him of a portion of the embarrassment which he expects to be the attendant of such awkwardness, many thousand insults of the kind passed unnoticed: — the Frenchman flattering himself that he had done a bold thing,—the Englishman a handsome one; whereas, had the character of the tread been distinctly understood, it would, no doubt, have been rewarded on the spot by *our* national method—a douse on the chops! However, be that as it may, my business is to record the result of one in which there was no misunderstanding; and, as some one has justly remarked, " when people are all of one mind, it is astonishing how well they agree."

It occurred at an early hour in the morning, at one of those seminaries for grown children so common in Paris, and the parties (a French officer and one of ours) agreed to meet at day-light, which left them but brief space for pre-paration, so that when they arrived on the ground, and their fighting irons were paraded, the Frenchman's were found to consist of a brace of pocket-pistols, with finger-sized barrels,— while our officer had a huge horse pistol, which he had borrowed from the quarter-mas-ter, and which looked, in the eyes of the astonished Frenchman, like a six-pounder, the bore of it being large enough to swallow the stocks, locks, and barrels of his brace, with the ball-bag and powder-horn into the bargain; and he, therefore, protested vehemently against the propriety of exposing himself to such fearful odds, which being readily admitted on the other side, they referred the decision to a halfpenny whether they should take alternate shots with the large, or one each with the small.

The Fates decreed in favour of the small arms; and, the combatants having taken their ground, they both fired at a given signal, when the result was that the Frenchman's pistol burst, and blew away his finger, while our man blew away his ramrod ; and as they had no longer the means of continuing the fight, they voted that they were a brace of good fellows, and after shaking the Frenchman by his other three fingers, our officer accompanied him home to breakfast.

SHOT THE SECOND.

Cannon-Law.

While stationed, in the province of Artois, with the Army of Occupation, one of our soldiers committed a most aggravated case of highway-robbery upon a Frenchwoman, for which he was tried by a court-martial, condemned, and suffered death within three days. About a fortnight after, when the whole affair had nearly been forgotten by us, the French report of the outrage, after having gone through its routine of the different official functionaries, made its ap-

pearance at our head-quarters, describing the
atrocious nature of the offence, and calling for
vengeance on the head of the offender. The
commander - in - chief's reply was, as usual,
short, but to the purpose :—The man was
hanged for it ten days ago.

SHOT THE THIRD.

Civil Law.

Whilst on the station mentioned in the foregoing anecdote, two of our medical officers
went in a gig, on a short tour, in the neighbourhood of our cantonments, and having un-
consciously passed the line of demarkation,
they were pulled up on their entrance into the
first town they came to, for the payment of the
usual toll ; but they claimed a right to be ex-
empted from it on the score of their being
officers of the Army of Occupation. The col-
lector of the customs, however, being of a dif-

ferent opinion, and finding his oratorical powers thrown away upon them, very prudently called to his aid one of those men-at-arms with which every village in France is so very considerately furnished. That functionary, squaring his cocked hat, giving his mustachoes a couple of twists, and announcing that he was as brave as a lion, as brave as the devil, and sundry other characters of noted courage, he, by way of illustration, drew his sword, and making half-a-dozen furious strokes at the paving stones, made the sparks fly from them like lightning. Seeing that the first half dozen had failed to extract the requisite quantity of sous, he was proceeding to give half-a-dozen more, but his sword broke at the first, and our two knights of the lancet, having fewer scruples about surrendering to him as an unarmed than an armed man, made no further difficulty in accompanying him to the municipal magistrate.

That worthy, after hearing both sides of the case with becoming gravity, finally sentenced our two travellers to pay for the repairs of

the sword which had been so courageously
broken in defence of their civic rights.

SHOT THE FOURTH.

Sword Law.

At the commencement of the battle of Waterloo, three companies of our riflemen held a
sand bank, in front of the position, and abreast
of La Haye Saint, which we clung to most
tenaciously, and it was not until we were stormed in front and turned in both flanks that we
finally left it. Previous to doing so, however,
a French officer rushed out of their ranks and
made a dash at one of ours, but neglecting the
prudent precaution of calculating the chances
of success before striking the first blow, it cost
him his life. The officer he stormed happened
to be a gigantic highlander about six feet and a
half—and, like most big men, slow to wrath, but

a fury when roused. The Frenchman held that in his hand which was well calculated to bring all sizes upon a level—a good small sword—but as he had forgotten to put on his spectacles, his first (and last) thrust passed by the body and lodged in the highlander's left arm. Saunders's blood was now up (as well as down) and with our then small regulation half-moon sabre, better calculated to shave a lady's-maid than a Frenchman's head, he made it descend on the pericranium of his unfortunate adversary with a force which snapped it at the hilt. His next dash was with his fist (and the hilt in it) smack in his adversary's face, which sent him to the earth ; and though I grieve to record it, yet as the truth must be told, I fear me that the chivalrous Frenchman died an ignominious death, viz. by a kick. But where one's own life is at stake, we must not be too particular.

Love Law.

Of all the evils with which a sober community can be cursed, there is none so great as
a guard-house; for while the notable house-wife
is superintending the scouring of her kitchen
coppers, and the worthy citizen is selling his
sweets, the daughters are as surely to be found
lavishing their's upon their gaudy neighbour,
while the nursery-maid standing a story higher
is to be seen sending her regards a step lower
—into the sentry-box.

Though many years have now passed away,
I remember as if but yesterday, my first guard
mounting, in a certain garrison town which shall
be nameless. After performing the first usual
routine of military duties, my next was, as a
matter of course, to reconnoitre the neighbourhood; for if a house happened to be within
range of the officer's beat, he seldom had to

look for an adventure in vain,—nor had I on the occasion alluded to. The station was in the centre of a populous city, the purlieus were genteel, and at the window of one of the opposite houses I soon descried a bevy of maidens who seemed to be regarding me with no small curiosity.

Eyes met eyes which looked again, and as all seemed to go merry as a marriage bell, I took out my pencil and motioned as if I would write, which meeting with an approving smile, I straightway indited an epistle suitable to the occasion, and shewing it to them when ready, I strolled past the door, where, as I expected, I found a fair hand which seemed to belong to nobody, in readiness to receive it.

In the course of a few minutes I received a note from the same mysterious hand, desiring to be informed for which of the group my last effusion was intended; and though the question was rather a puzzler to a person who had never seen them before, and, even then, too far off to be able to distinguish whether their eyes were

green or yellow, yet I very judiciously requested
that my correspondent would accept it on her
own account. It was arranged accordingly,
and her next epistle, while it preached prudence and discretion, desired that I should
come to the door at eleven at night when she
would have an opportunity of speaking to me.

It may be imagined that time flew on leaden
wings until the arrival of the appointed hour,
when proceeding as directed, I found the door
ajar, and the vision of the hand, now with
a body in the back ground, beckoning me to
enter. Following the invitation the door was
gently closed, and I was soon in a large dimly
lighted hall, by the side of my fair incog-
nita, with my hand clasped in hers. But ah
me! I had barely time to unburthen myself of
a hurricane of sighs (enough to have blown a
fire out) and to give one chaste salute, when
papa's well-known knock was heard at the door
and dissolved the charm.

In an agony of affright my fair friend desired
me to run up stairs to the first landing, and as

I valued my life, not to stir from it until she should come to fetch me.

Misfortunes they say seldom come single, and so I found it, for I had scarcely reached the desired place when the voice of the sentry thundered, " Guard, turn out!" and conveyed to me the very pleasant information that the grand rounds approached, while I, the officer of the guard, was absent, the captive of a damsel. I was in a precious scrape; for, prior to the arrival of the other evil, I held it to be somewhat more than doubtful whether I was reserved for a kiss or a kick, but the odds were now two to one in favour of the latter, for if I did not find my way outside the walls within three quarters of a minute, it was quite certain that if I failed to receive what was due to me inside the house I should catch it outside, by getting kicked from the service. My case was therefore desperate, and as the voice of papa was still heard at the stair-foot and precluded the possibility of bolting undetected by the door, my only alternative was the stair window.

The field officer was passing under it as I threw up the sash, and though the distance to the ground loomed fearfully long there was no time for deliberation, but bundling out, and letting myself down by the hands as far as I could, I took my chance of the remainder and came down on the pavement with such a tremendous clatter that I thought I had been shivered to atoms. The noise fortunately startled the field officer's horse, so that it was as much as he could do to keep his seat for the moment, which gave me time to gather myself up; when, telling him that in my hurry to get to my place before him, I had stumbled against a lamp post and fallen, the affair passed away without further notice, but my aching bones, for many an after-day, would not permit me to forget the adventure of that night.

In my next turn for guard at the same place I got a glimpse of my fair friend, and but for once. I saw on my arrival that the family were in marching order, and my old acquaintance, the hand, soon after presented me with a billet announcing their immediate departure for the season, to a distant watering place. She lamented the accident which she feared had befallen me, and as she thought it probable that we would never meet again, she begged that I would forgive and look upon it merely as the badinage of a giddy girl.

SHOT THE SIXTH.

At a sore subject.

" They who can feel for other's woes should ne'er have cause to mourn their own ! "so sayeth the poet, and so should I say if I saw them feeling ; but I have found such a marvellous scarcity of those tender-hearted subjects on the field of battle, that, in good sooth, if the soldier had not a tear to shed for his own woes, he stood a very good chance of dying unwept, which may either be considered a merry or a

dreary end, according to the notion of the individual.

In taking a comparative view of the *comforts*
attending a sea and land fight, I know not what
evils our nautical brethren may have to contend
against, which we have not; but they have this
advantage over us—that, whatever may be the
fate of the day, they have their bed and breakfast, and their wounds are promptly attended to.
This shot, be it observed, is especially fired at
the wounded.

When a man is wounded the corps he belongs
to is generally in action, and cannot spare from
the ranks the necessary assistance, so that he
is obliged to be left to the tender mercies of
those who follow after, and they generally pay
him the attention due to a mad dog, by giving
him as wide a berth as they possibly can—so
that he often lies for days in the field without
assistance of any kind.

Those who have never witnessed such scenes
will be loth to believe that men's hearts can get

so steeled ; but so it is—the same chance befals the officer as the soldier, and one anecdote will illustrate both.

At the battle of Vittoria one of our officers was disabled by a shot through the leg, but having contrived to drag himself to a road-side, he laid himself down there, in the hope that, among the passing thousands, some good Samaritan might be found with compassion enough to bind up his wound, and convey him to a place of shelter.

The rear of a battle is generally a queer place —the day is won and lost there a dozen times, unknown to the actual combatants—fellows who have never seen an enemy in the field, are there to be seen flourishing their drawn swords, and " cutting such fantastic tricks before high heaven, as make angels weep," while others are flying as if pursued by legions of demons; and, in short, while every thing is going on in front with the order and precision of a field-day, in rear every thing is confusion worse confounded.

When my wounded friend took post on the road-side, it was in the midst of a panic amongst the followers of the army, caused by an imaginary charge of cavalry—he tried in vain, for a length of time, to attract the notice of somebody, when his eyes were at length regaled by a staff surgeon of his acquaintance, who approached amid the crowd of fugitives, and, having no doubt but he would at length receive the requisite attention, he hailed him by name as soon as he came within reach. The person hailed, pulled up, with " Ah! my dear fellow, how do you do? I hope you are not badly hit?" " I can't answer for that," replied my friend, " all I know is, that my leg is bleeding profusely, and until some good-natured person dresses it and assists me to remove, here I must lie!" " Ah! that's right," returned the other, " keep yourself quiet—this is only an affair of cavalry—so that you may make yourself quite comfortable," and, clapping spurs to his horse, he was out of sight in a moment!

The next known character who presented

himself was a volunteer, at that time attached
to the regiment—an eccentric sort of a gentleman, but one who had a great deal of method in
his eccentricity—for, though he always went
into battle with us, I know not how it happened, but no one ever saw him again until it
was all over—he must have been an especial
favourite of the fickle goddess—for, by his own
shewing, his absence from our part of the battle
was always occasioned by his accidentally falling in with some other regiment which had lost
all its officers, and, after rallying and leading
them on to the most brilliant feat of the day,
he, with the modesty becoming a hero, left them
alone in their glory—in ignorance of the person
to whom they owed so much, while he retired
to his humble position as a volunteer !

On the occasion referred to, however, in place
of being at the head of a regiment and leading
them on to the front, he was at the head of half
a dozen horses, which he had contrived to scrape
together in the field, and was leading them the
other road. As soon as he had descried my

L

wounded friend he addressed him as did the doctor—was remarkably glad to see him, and hoped he was not badly hit—and, having received a similar reply, he declared that he was very sorry to hear it—*very*—" but," added he, " as you are lying there, at all events, perhaps you will be good enough to hold these horses for me until I return, for I know where I can get about as many more !"

Patience had not then ceased to be a virtue— and, lest my readers should think that I am drawing too largely on theirs, I shall resume the thread of my narrative.

CHAP. IX.

A bishop's gathering.—Volunteers for a soldier's love, with a portrait of the lover.—Burning a bivouac.—Old invented thrashing machines and baking concerns.—A flying Padre taking a shot flying.

Soon after the battle of Fuentes Lord Wellington was again called to the south, leaving us with a burning desire to follow, which was eventually gratified; for, after various coquettish movements between us and the enemy, which carried us in retreat near to Sabugal, we, at length, received an order for the south; and, leaving our adversaries to do that which might seem best unto them, we were all at once helm up for the other side of the Tagus.

On our way there we halted a night at Castello Branco, and hearing that the Bishop's garden was open for inspection, and well worth the seeing, I went with a brother-officer to reconnoitre it.

Throughout the country which we had been traversing for a season, the ravages of the contending armies had swept the fruits, flowers, and even the parent stems, from the face of the earth, as if such things had never been; and it is, therefore, difficult to convey an idea of the gratification we experienced in having our senses again regaled with all that was delightful in either, and in admirable order.

Beauty, in whatever shape it comes before us, is almost irresistible, and the worthy prelate's oranges proved quite so; for they looked so brightly yellow—so plumply ripe—and the trees groaned with their load, as if praying for relief, that with hearts framed as ours, so sensitively alive to nature's kindlier feelings, it was impossible to refuse the appeal.

Stolen kisses, they say, are the sweetest, and

besides, as there might have been some impropriety in pressing the oranges to our lips so publicly, we were at some loss to provide for their transfer to a suitable place, as our dress was pocketless, and fitted as tight as a glove; but we contrived to stow away about a dozen each in our then sugar-loaf-shaped regimental caps, and placing them carefully on the head, we marched off as stifly as a brace of grenadiers.

As the devil would have it, however, in traversing the palace-hall, we encountered the Bishop himself, and as it was necessary that the compliments of the season should pass between us, it was rather an awkward meeting; I was myself alive to the consequences of having more brains above the head than in it, and, therefore, confined myself to the stiff soldier's salute; but my companion, unluckily, forgot his load, and in politely returning the prelate's bow, sent his cap and oranges rolling at his feet, while his face shone as a burnt offering at the same shrine!

The Bishop gave a benevolent smile, and after very good naturedly assisting the youth to collect the scattered fruit, he politely wished us a good morning, leaving us not a little ashamed of ourselves, and deeply impressed with a sense of his gentleman-like demeanour and amiable disposition.

Our third march from Castello Branco brought us to Portalegre, where we halted for some days.

In a former chapter, I have given the Portuguese national character, such as I found it generally,—but in nature there are few scenes so blank as to have no sunny side, and throughout that kingdom, the romantic little town of Portalegre still dwells the greenest spot on memory's waste.

Unlike most other places in that devoted land, it had escaped the vengeful visit of their ruthless foe, and having, therefore, no fatal remembrance to cast its shade over the future, the inhabitants received us as if we had been beings of a superior order, to whom they were indebted for all the blessings they enjoyed, and showered their sweets upon us accordingly.

In three out of four of my sojourns there, a friend and I had the good fortune to be quartered in the same house. The family consisted of a mother and two daughters, who were very good-looking and remarkably kind. Our return was ever watched for with intense interest, and when they could not command sufficient influence with the local authorities to have the house reserved, they nevertheless contrived to squeeze us in; for when people are in a humour to be pleased with each other, small space suffices for their accommodation.

Such uniform kindness on their part, it is unnecessary to say, did not fail to meet a suitable return on ours. We had few opportunities of falling in with things that were rich and rare, (if I except such *jewels* as those just mentioned,) yet were we always stumbling over something or other, which was carefully preserved for our next happy meeting; and whether they were gems or gew-gaws, they were alike valued for the sake of the donors.

The kindness shown by one family to two particular individuals goes, of course, for nothing beyond its value; but the feeling there seemed to be universal.

Our usual morning's amusement was to visit one or other of the convents, and having ascertained the names of the different pretty nuns, we had only to ring the bell, and request the pleasure of half-an-hour's conversation with one of the prettiest amongst them, to have it indulged; and it is curious enough that I never yet asked a nun, or an attendant of a nunnery, if she would elope with me, that she did not immediately consent,—and that, too, unconditionally.

My invitations to that effect were not general, but, on the contrary, remarkably particular; and to show that in accepting it they meant no joke, they invariably pointed out the means, by telling me that they were strictly watched at that time, but if I returned privately, a week or two after the army had passed, they could very easily arrange the manner of their escape.

I take no credit to myself for any preference shewn, for if there be any truth in my looking-glass—and it was one of the most flattering I could find—their discriminating powers would entitle them to small credit for any partiality shewn to me individually; and while it was no compliment, therefore, to me, or to the nunnery, it must necessarily be due to nature, as showing that the good souls were overflowing with the milk of human kindness, and could not say nay while they possessed the powers of pleasing : for, as far as I have compared notes with my companions, the feeling seemed to have been general.

On quitting Portalegre, we stopped, the next night, at Aronches, a small miserable walled town, with scarcely a house in it that would entitle the holder to vote on a ten shilling fran-chise; and on the night following we went into

bivouac, on Monte Reguingo, between Campo
Mayor and the Caya, where we remained a
considerable time. We were there, as our gallant historian (Napier) tells us, in as judicious
but, at the same time, in as desperate a position
as any that Lord Wellington had held during
the war; yet, I am free to say, however, that
none of us knew any thing at all about the
matter, and cared still less. We there held, as
we ever did, the most unbounded confidence in
our chief, and a confidence in ourselves, fed by
continued success, which was not to be shaken;
so that we were at all times ready for any thing,
and reckless of every thing. The soldiers had
become so inured to toil and danger that they
seemed to have set disease, the elements, and
the enemy alike at defiance. Head-aches and
heart-aches were unknown amongst them, and
whether they slept under a roof, a tent, or the
open sky, or whether they amused themselves
with a refreshing bath in a stream, or amused
the enemy with a shot, was all a matter of indif-

ference. I do not eulogize our own men at the expense of others, for although the light division stood on that particular post alone, our chief confidence originated in the hope and belief that every division in the army was animated by the same spirit.

The day after our taking post at Reguingo, notwithstanding my boasted daring, we were put to the rout by an unlooked-for enemy, namely, a fire in the bivouac;—a scorching sun had dried up the herbage, and some of the campfires communicated with the long grass on which we were lodged; the fresh summer-breeze wafted the ground flame so rapidly through the bivouac that before all the arms and accoutrements could be removed, many of the men's pouches were blown-up, and caused some accidents.

I believe it is not generally, and cannot be too well known to military men, that this is a measure which is very often had recourse to by an enemy, (when the wind favours,) to dislodge a post from a field of standing corn or long

grass ; and the only way to counteract it is, for
the officer commanding the post to fire the grass
immediately behind him, so that by the time
the enemy's fire has burnt up, his own will
have gone away in proportion, and left a secure
place for him to stand on, without losing much
ground.

Our bivouac at Monte Reguingo abounded
in various venomous reptiles, and it is curious
enough to think that amongst the thousands of
human beings sleeping in the same bed and at
their mercy, one rarely or never heard of an
injury done by them.

A decayed tree full of holes, against which
the officers of our company had built their straw
hut, was quite filled with snakes, and I have
often seen fellows three feet long winding their
way through the thatch, and voting themselves
our companions at all hours, but the only inconvenience we experienced was in a sort of feeling
that we would rather have had the hut to ourselves.

One morning in turning over a stone on which

my head had rested all night, I saw a scorpion with the tail curled over his back looking me fiercely in the face; and though not of much use, I made it a rule thereafter to take a look at the other side of my pillow before I went to sleep, whenever I used a stone one.

An officer in putting on his shoe one morning, found that he had squeezed a scorpion to death in the toe of it. That fellow must have been caught napping, or he certainly would have resisted the intruder.

The only thing in the shape of an accident from reptiles that I remember ever having occurred in our regiment was to a soldier who had somehow swallowed a lizard. He knew not when or how, and the first hint he had of the tenement being so occupied, was in being troubled with internal pains and spitting of blood, which continued for many months, in spite of all the remedies that were administered. But a powerful emetic eventually caused him to be delivered of as ugly a child of the kind as one would wish to look at, about three inches long. I believe that Dr. Burke, late of the Rifles, has it still preserved.

In that neighbourhood I was amused in observing the primitive method adopted by the farmers in thrashing their corn,—namely, in placing it on a hard part of the public road and driving some bullocks backwards and forwards through it; and for winnowing, they tossed it in a sieve and trusted to the winds to do the needful. Notwithstanding the method, however, they contrived to shew us good looking bread in that part of the world—as white as a confectioner's seed cake — and though the devil take such seeds as these sons of cows had contrived to grind up with the flour, yet it was something like the cooking on board ship; we ought to have been thankful for the good which the Gods provided and asked no questions.

In July, the breaking up of the assembled armies which had so long menaced us, sent our division again stretching off to the north in pursuit of fresh game. The weather was so intensely hot, that it was thought advisable to perform the greater part of our marches during the night. I can imagine few cases, however, in which a night march can prove in any way advantageous; for unless the roads are remarkably good, it requires double time to perform them. The men go stumbling along half asleep, and just begin to brighten up when their permitted hour of repose arrives. The scorching sun, too, murders sleep, and of our ten or twelve days' marching on that occasion, I scarcely ever slept at all. I have always been of opinion that if men who are inured to fatigue are suffered to have a decent allowance of repose during the night, that you may do what you like with them during the day, let the climate or the weather be what it may.

I remember having been at that time in possession of a small black pony, and like the old man and his ass, it might have admitted of a dispute among the spectators which of us ought to have carried the other, but to do myself justice I rarely put him to the inconvenience of carrying anything beyond my boat-cloak, blanket, &c.; but one morning before day-light, in stumbling along through one of those sleepy marches, my charger, following at the length of the bridle-rein, all at once shot past me as if he had been fired out of a mortar, and went heels over head, throwing a complete somerset and upsetting two of the men in his headlong career. I looked at the fellow in the utmost astonishment to see whether he was in joke or earnest, thinking that I had by accident got hold of one of Astley's cast-off's, who was shewing me some of his old stage tricks, but when he got up, he gave himself a shake and went quietly on as usual, so that it must have been nothing beyond a dreaming caper, seeing that he was not much given to the exhibition of feats of agility in his waking moments.

On reaching our destination in the north, our division took up a more advanced position than before, and placed the garrison of Ciudad Rodrigo under blockade.

In the first village we occupied (Mortiago) the

only character worthy of note was a most active half-starved curate, whose duty it was to marry and to bury every body within a wide range, besides performing the usual services in sundry chapels in that and the adjoining villages. He was so constantly at a gallop on horseback in pursuit of his avocations that we dubbed him the *Padrè volante* (the flying parson.) We did there, as in all the Spanish villages the moment we took possession, levelled the ground at the end of the church, and with wooden bats cut out in the shape of rackets, got up something like an apology for that active and delightful game.

Our greatest enjoyment there was to catch the Padrè in one of his leisure moments and to get him to join in the amusement, of which he was remarkably fond, and he was no sooner enlisted, than it became the malicious aim of every one to send the ball against his lank ribs. Whenever he saw that it was done intentionally, however, he made no hesitation in shying his bat at the offender; but he was a good-natured soul, as were also his tormentors, so that every thing passed off as was intended.

The Padrè in addition to his other accomplishments was a sportsman, and as he was possessed of a pointer dog (a companion which, as we had more mouths than food, we were obliged to deny ourselves), his company in the field on that account was in great request; whatever his feats might have been there however, he generally came off but second best. I remember that two of our gentlemen accompanied him the first day, and when they sprung the first covey, the Padrè's bird, out of the three shots, was the only one that came to the ground; but notwithstanding, one of the officers immediately ran up and very coolly placed it in his own bag. The Padrè ran up too, and stood gaping open-mouthed thinking he had pocketed the bird in joke; however, the other went on deliberately loading as if all had been right. Meanwhile, the other officer coming up, said, " Why, S. that was not your bird, it is the Padrè's!" " My dear sir," he replied, " I know it is not

my bird, but do you suppose that I would allow
a fellow like that to think that he had killed a
bird? My good sir, I would not allow him
to suppose for one moment that he had even
fired at it!"

CHAP. X.

Shewing how a volunteer may not be what Doctor Johnson
made him.—A mayor's nest.—Cupping.—The Author's
reasons for punishing the world with a book.—And some
volunteers of the right sort.

WHEN we next changed our quarter we found
the new one peopled exclusively by old wives
and their husbands, and, as the enemy were at
a distance, we should certainly have gone defunct through sheer ennui, had not fortune sent
us a fresh volunteer—a regular " broth of a
boy," from the Emerald Isle, who afforded
ample scope for the exercise of our mischievous
propensities during our hours of idleness.

A volunteer—be it known to all who know it

not—is generally a young man with some pretensions to gentility—and while, with some, those pretensions are so admirably disguised as to be scarcely visible to the naked eye, in others they are conspicuous; but, in either case, they are persons who, being without the necessary influence to obtain a commission at home, get a letter of introduction to the commander of the forces in the field, who, if he approves, attaches them to regiments, and, while they are treated as gentlemen out of the field, they receive the pay, and do the duty of private soldiers in it. In every storming party or service of danger, in which any portion of a regiment is engaged, if a volunteer is attached to it, he is expected to make one of the number, and, if a bullet does not provide for him in the meantime, he eventually succeeds to the commission of some officer who has fallen in action.

Tommy Dangerfield, the hero of my tale, was, no doubt, (as we all are,) the hero of his mother—in stature he was middle sized—rather bull shouldered, and walked with bent knees—

his face was a fresh good-natured one, but with the usual sinister cast in the eye worn by common Irish country countenances—in short, Tommy was rather a good-looking, and, in reality, not a bad, fellow, and the only mistake which he seemed to have made, was in the choice of his profession, for which his general appearance and his ideas altogether disqualified him—nevertherless, had he fallen into other hands it is possible that he might have passed muster with tolerable repute until the termination of the war; but I don't know how it was, nor do I know whether we differed from other regiments in the same respect, but our first and most uncharitable aim was to discover the weak points of every fresh arrival, and to attack him through them. If he had redeeming qualities, he, of course, came out scatheless, but, if not, he was dealt with most unmercifully. Poor Tommy had none such—he was weak on all sides, and therefore went to the wall.

At the time he joined, we were unusually situated with regard to the enemy, for, on ordi-

nary occasions, we had their sentries opposite
to ours within a few hundred yards; but, at that
period, we had the French garrison of Ciudad
Rodrigo behind us, with the 52d regiment between ; while the nearest enemy in our front was
distant some ten or twelve miles—nevertheless,
our first essay was to impress Tommy with a
notion that our village was a fortified place, and
that we were closely blockaded on all sides—and
it became our daily amusement to form a reconnoitring party to endeavour to penetrate beyond
the posts—which posts, be it remarked, were
held by a few of our own men, disguised for
the purpose, and posted at the out-skirts of the
village wood.

Tommy, though not a desperate character,
shewed no want of pluck—wherever we went he
followed, and wherever we fled he led the way!

On the first occasion of the kind we got him
on horseback, and conducting him through the
wood until we received the expected volley, we
took to our heels in the hope that he would get
unseated in the flight, but he held on like grim

death, and arrived in the village with the loss of his cap only. It was, however, brought to him in due time by an old rifleman of the name of Brotherwood, who had commanded the enemy on that occasion, but who claimed peculiar merit in its recovery; and, having taken the opportunity of cutting a hole in it as if a ball had passed through, he got a dollar for the cut!

Poor Tommy, from that time, led the life of the devil—he could not shew his nose outside his own house that he was not fired at—and whenever we made up a larger party to shew him more of the world it was only to lead him into further mischief.

I was some time after this removed into the left wing of our regiment, which belonged to a different brigade, so that I ceased to be a daily witness of his torments, though aware that they went on as theretofore.

Tommy continued to rub on for a considerable time. Death had become busy in our ranks—first, by the siege and storming of Ciudad Rodrigo, and immediately after, by that of Badajos.

I had heard little or nothing of him during those stirring events of real war—and it was not until the morning after the storming of Badajos that he again came under my notice—from having heard that he had been missing the night before. I there saw him turn up, like a half-drowned rat, covered with mud and wet, which looked very much as if he had passed the night in the inundation, adjoining the breach, up to his neck in the water, and probably a little deeper at times, when the fire-balls were flying thickest. He nevertheless contrived to hold on yet a little longer—one day, (agreeably to order,) taking post in the middle of a river, with his face towards Ispahan, to watch the enemy in that direction—and the next day, in conformity with the same orders, applying to the quarter-master-general for a route for himself and party to go to Kamskatcha to recruit, he got so bewildered that he could not distinguish between a sham and a real order, and, at last, when in the face of the enemy, in front of Salamanca, he absolutely refused to take the duty for

M

which he had been ordered, and was consequently obliged to cut.

It was the best thing that could have happened both for him and the service; for, as
I said before, he had mistaken his profession,
and as he was yet but a youth, it is to be hoped
that he afterwards stumbled upon the right one.

Atalya, which we now occupied, is a mountain village about half a league in front of the
Vadillo. The only amusing characters we found
in it were the pigs. I know not whether any
process was resorted to in the mornings to en-
tice them from their homes to grub up the
falling acorns from the beautiful little evergreen
oaks which adorned the hills above, but it was a
great scene every evening at sunset to go to the
top of the village, and see about five hundred
of them coming thundering down the face of
the mountain at full speed, and each galloping
in to his own door.

We had been a considerable time there before
we discovered that the neighbourhood could
furnish metal more attractive, but a shooting

excursion at last brought us acquainted with the Quinta Horquera (I think it was called), a very respectable farm-house, situated on a tongue of land formed by the junction of another mountain stream with the Vadillo.

The house itself was nothing out of the common run, but its inmates were, for we found it occupied by the chief magistrate of Ciudad Rodrigo, with his wife and daughter, and two young female relatives. He himself was a staunch friend of his country, and when the fortress of Rodrigo fell into the hands of the French, rather than live in communion with them, he retired with his family to that remote property, in the hope that as it was so much out of the way he might rest there in peace and security until circumstances enabled him to resume his position in society as a true and loyal Spaniard; but as the sequel will shew, he had reckoned without his host, for with a British regiment in the neighbourhood, and his house filled with young ladies he was an unreasonable man to expect peace there, and the enemy also by and bye came down upon him, as if to prove that his notions of security were equally fallacious.

Don Miguel himself was a splendid ruin of a man of three score, of a majestic figure, regular features, and stern dark Castilian countenance. He was kind and amusing withal, for though his own face was forbidden to smile, yet he seemed to enjoy it in others, and did all in his power to promote amusement, that is, as much as a Spaniard ever does.

His wife was very tall and very slender—the skin of her pale fleshless face fitting so tight as to make it look like a pin-head. She was very passive and very good-natured, her other day having long passed by.

Their only daughter was a woman about twenty-eight years of age, with rather a dull pock-pitted countenance, and a tall, stout, clumsy figure. She had very little of the Spaniard in her composition, but was nevertheless a kind good-natured girl. Her relatives, however, were metal of another sort: the eldest was a remarkably well made plump little figure, with a fair complexion, natural curly hair, and a face full of dimples which shewed eternal sunshine; while her sister, as opposite as day from night, shewed the flashing dark eye, sallow complexion, and the light sylph-like figure for which her country-women are so remarkable. To look at her was to see a personification of that beautiful description of Byron's in his first canto of Childe Harold —

" Yet are Spain's maids no race of Amazons,
But formed for all the witching arts of love!"

Their house, under the circumstances in which we were placed, became an agreeable lounge for many of us for a month or two, for though the sports of the field, with the limited means at our disposal, formed our daily amusement, we always contrived that it should terminate somewhere in the neighbourhood of the Quinta, where we were sure of three things—a hearty welcome, a dish of conversation, and another of chestnuts fried in hog's-lard, with a glass of aguadente to wind up with, which, after the fatigues of the day, carried us comfortably home to our more substantial repast, with a few little pleasing recollections to dream about.

The French marshal, as if envious of our enjoyments, meagre as they were, put a sudden stop to them. His advance, however, was not so rapid but that we were enabled to give our first care towards providing for the safety of our friends of the Quinta, by assisting them with the means of transporting themselves to a more remote glen in the mountains, before it was necessary to look to our own, and

> Although the links of love that morn
> Which War's rude hands had asunder torn

had not been patent ones, yet did it savour somewhat of chivalric times when we had been one evening in the field in the front of the Quinta sporting with the young and the lovely of the land, as if wars and rumours of wars were to be heard of no more.

I say I felt it rather queerish or so, to be

spreading down my boat-cloak for a bed in the same field the next night, with an enemy in my front, for so it was, and to find myself again before day-light next morning, from my cold clay couch, gazing at the wonderful comet of 1811, that made such capital claret, and wishing that he would wag his fiery tale a little nearer to my face, for it was so stiff with hoar frost that I dared neither to laugh nor cry for fear of breaking it.

We passed yet another night in the same field hallowed by such opposite recollections; but next day, independently of the gathered strength of the enemy in our front, we found a fight of some magnitude going on behind us, the combat of Elbodon; and our major-general, getting alarmed at last at his own temerity, found a sleeping place for us, some distance in the rear, in a hollow, where none but the comet and its companions might be indulged with a look.

Our situation was more than ticklish—with an enemy on three sides and an almost impassable mountain on the fourth—but starting with

the lark next morning and passing through Ro-
bledillo, we happily succeeded in joining the
army in front of Guinaldo in the afternoon, to
the no small delight of his Grace of Wellington,
whose judicious and daring front with half the
enemy's numbers, had been our salvation. And
it must no doubt have been a mortifying reflection to our divisional chief, to find that his
obstinacy and disobedience of orders had not
only placed his own division, but that of the
whole army in such imminent peril.

Marmont had no doubt a laurel-wreath in
embryo for the following day, but he had allowed *his* day to go by; the night was ours and
we used it, so that when day-light broke, he
had nothing but empty field-works to wreak his
vengeance on. He followed us along the road,
with some sharp partial fighting at one or two
places, and there seemed a probability of his
coming on to the position in which Lord Wellington felt disposed to give him battle; but a
scarcity of provisions forced him to retrace his
steps, and break up to a certain extent for the

subsistence of his army, while our retreat terminated at Soita, which it appeared was about
the spot on which Lord Wellington had determined to make a stand.

I shall ever remember our night at Soita for
one thing. The commissariat had been about
to destroy a cask of rum in the course of that
day's retreat, when at the merciful intercession
of one of my brother officers, it was happily
spared and turned over to his safe keeping, and
he shewed himself deserving of the trust, for
by wonderful dexterity and management, he
contrived to get it wheeled along to our resting-
place, when establishing himself under the
awning of a splendid chestnut-tree, he hung out
the usual emblem of its being the head-quarters
of a highland chief—not for the purpose of
scaring way-fairers as erst did his forefathers
of yore, to exclude the worthy Baillie Nicol
Jarvie from the clachan of Aberfoyle—but for
the more hospitable one of inviting them to be
partakers thereof; and need I add that among
the many wearers of empty calabashes which

the chances of war had there assembled around him, the call was cheerfully responded to, and a glorious group very quickly assembled.

The morrow promised to be a bloody one; but we cared not for the morrow:—" sufficient for the day is the evil thereof:"—the song and the jest went merrily round, and, if the truth must be told, I believe that though we carried our cups to the feast, we all went back in them, and with the satisfaction of knowing that we had relieved our gallant chieftain of all further care respecting the contents of the cask.

The enemy having withdrawn the same night, we retraced our steps, next day, to our former neighbourhood; and though we were occasionally stirred up and called together by the menacing attitudes of our opponents, yet we remained the unusually long period of nearly three months without coming again into actual contact with them.

No officer during that time had one fraction to rub against another; and when I add that our paunches were nearly as empty as our

pockets, it will appear almost a libel upon common sense to say that we enjoyed it; yet so it
was,—our very privations were a subject of pride
and boast to us, and there still continued to be
an *esprit de corps*,—a buoyancy of feeling
animating all, which nothing could quell; we
were alike ready for the field or for frolic, and
when not engaged in the one, went headlong
into the other.

Ah me! when I call to mind that our chief
support in those days of trial was the anticipated delight of recounting those tales in after
years, to wondering and admiring groups around
our domestic hearths, in merry England; and
when I find that so many of these after years
have already passed, and that the folks who
people these present years, care no more about
these dear-bought tales of former ones than if
they were spinning-wheel stories of some " auld
wife ayont the fire;" I say it is not only enough to
make me inflict them with a book, as I have done,
but it makes me wish that I had it all to do over

again; and I think it would be very odd if I would not do exactly as I have done, for I knew no happier times, and they were their own reward!

It is worthy of remark that Lord Wellington, during the time I speak of, had made his arrangements for pouncing upon the devoted fortress of Ciudad Rodrigo, with such admirable secresy, that his preparations were not even known to his own army.

I remember, about a fortnight before the siege commenced, hearing that some gabions and fascines were being made in the neighbourhood, but it was spoken of as a sort of sham preparation, intended to keep the enemy on the *qui vive*, as it seemed improbable that he would dare to invest a fortress in the face of an army which he had not force enough to meet in the field, unless on some select position; nor was it until the day before we opened the trenches that we became quite satisfied that he was in earnest.

The sieges, stormings, and capture of Ciudad

Rodrigo and Badajos followed hard on each other's heels; and as I gave a short detail of the operations in my former volume, it only remains for me now to introduce such anecdotes and remarks as were there omitted.

The garrison of Ciudad was weak in number, but had a superabundant store of ammunition, which was served out to us with a liberal hand; yet, curious enough, except what was bestowed on the working parties, (and that was plenty in all conscience,) the greater portion of what was intended for the supporting body was expended in air, for they never seemed to have discovered the true position of the besieging force; and though some few of us, in the course of each night, by chance-shots, got transferred from natural to eternal sleep, yet their shells were chiefly employed in the ploughing-up of a hollow way between two hills, where we were supposed to have been, and which they did most effectually at their own cost.

When our turn of duty came for the trenches, however, we never had reason to consider ourselves neglected, but, on the contrary, could well spare what was sent at random.

I have often heard it disputed whether the most daring deeds are done by men of good or bad repute, but I never felt inclined to give either a preference over the other, for I have seen the most desperate things done by both. I remember one day during the siege that a shell pitched in the trenches within a few yards of a noted bad character of the 52d regiment, who, rather than take the trouble of leaping out of the trench until it had exploded, went very deliberately up, took it in his arms, and pitched it outside, obliging those to jump back who had there taken shelter from it.

A wild young officer, whose eccentricities and death, at Waterloo, were noticed in my former volume, was at that time at variance with his father on the subject of pecuniary matters, and in mounting the breach, at Ciudad, sword in hand, while both sides were falling thick and fast, he remarked to a brother-officer alongside of him, in his usual jocular way, " Egad, if I had my old father here now, I think I should be able to bring him to terms !"

Nothing shows the spirit of daring and inherent bravery of the British soldier so much as in the calling for a body of volunteers for any desperate service. In other armies, as Napier justly remarks, the humblest helmet may catch a beam of glory; but in ours, while the subaltern commanding the forlorn hope may look for death or a company, and the field-officer commanding the stormers an additional step by brevet, to the other officers and soldiers who volunteer on that desperate service, no hope is held out—no reward given; and yet there were as many applicants for a place in the ranks as if it led to the highest honours and rewards.

At the stormings of Badajos and St. Sebastian I happened to be the adjutant of the regiment, and had the selection of the volunteers on those occasions, and I remember that there was as much anxiety expressed, and as much interest made by all ranks to be appointed to the post of honour, as if it had been sinecure situations, in place of death-warrants, which I had at my disposal.

For the storming of St. Sebastian, the numbers from our battalion were limited to twenty-five; and in selecting the best characters out of those who offered themselves, I rejected an Irishman of the name of Burke, who, although he had been on the forlorn hope both at Ciudad and Badajos, and was a man of desperate bravery, I knew to be one of those wild untameable animals that, the moment the place was carried, would run into every species of excess.

The party had been named two days before they were called for, and Burke besieged my tent night and day, assuring me all the while that unless he was suffered to be of the party, the place would not be taken! I was forced at last to yield, after receiving an application in his behalf from the officer who was to command the party; and he was one of the very few of that gallant little band who returned to tell the story.

Nor was that voracious appetite for fire-eating

confined to the private soldier, for it extended alike to all ranks. On the occasion just alluded to, our quota, as already stated, was limited to a subaltern's command of twenty-five men ; and as the post of honour was claimed by the senior lieutenant, (Percival,) it in a manner shut the mouths of all the juniors ; yet were there some whose mouths would not be shut,—one in particular (Lieutenant H.) who had already seen enough of fighting to satisfy the mind of any reasonable man, for he had stormed and bled at Ciudad Rodrigo, and he had stormed at Badajos, not to mention his having had his share in many, and not nameless battles, which had taken place in the interim ; yet nothing would satisfy him but that he must draw his sword in that also.

Our colonel was too heroic a soul himself to check a feeling of that sort in those under him, and he very readily obtained the necessary permission to be a volunteer along with the party. Having settled his temporal affairs, namely, willing away his pelisse, jacket, two pairs of

trousers, and sundry nether garments,—and
however trifling these bequests may appear to a
military youth of the present day, who happens
to be reconnoitring a merchant tailor's settlement
in St. James's Street, yet let me tell him that,
at the time I speak of, they were valued as
highly as if they had been hundreds a year in
reversion.

The prejudice against will-making by soldiers
on service is so strong, that had H. been a rich
man in place of a poor one, he must have
died on the spot for doing what was accounted
infinitely more desperate than storming a breach;
but his poverty seemed to have been his salvation, for he was only half killed,—a ball entered
under his eye, passed down the roof of the
mouth, through the palate, entered again at the
collar-bone, and was cut out at the shoulder-
blade. He never again returned to his regiment, but I saw him some years after, in his
native country (Ireland), in an active situation,
and, excepting that he had gotten an ugly mark

on his countenance, and his former manly voice had dwindled into a less commanding one, he seemed as well as ever I saw him.

Will-making, as already hinted at, was, in the face of the enemy, reckoned the most daring of all daring deeds, for the doer was always considered a doomed man, and it was but too often verified—not but that the same fatality must have marked him out without it; but so strong was the prejudice generally on that subject that many a goodly estate has, in consequence, passed into what, under other circumstances, would have been forbidden hands.

On the subject of presentiments of death in going into battle, I have known as many instances of falsification as verification. To the latter the popular feeling naturally clings as the more interesting of the two; but I am inclined to think that the other would preponderate if the account could be justly rendered. The officer alluded to may be taken as a specimen of the former—he had been my messmate and companion at the sieges and stormings of both

Ciudad and Badajos—and on the morning after the latter, he told me that he had had a presentiment that he would have fallen the night before, though he had been ashamed to confess it sooner—and yet to his credit be it spoken, so far from wishing to avoid, he coveted the post of danger—as his duty for that day would have led him to the trenches, but he exchanged with another officer, on purpose to ensure himself a place in the storm.

Of my own feelings on the point in consideration, I am free to say that, while I have been engaged in fifty actions, in which I have neither had the time, nor taken the trouble to ask myself any questions on the subject, but encountered them in whatever humour I happened to be—yet, in many others, (the eve of pitched battles,) when the risk was imminent, and certain that one out of every three must go to the ground, I have asked myself the question, " Do I feel like a *dead* man ?" but I was invariably answered point blank, " *No !*" And yet must I still look like a superstitious character, when I declare that the only time that I ever went into action, labouring under a regular depression of spirits, was on the evening on which the musket ball felt my head at Foz d'Aronce.

But to return to the storming of Ciudad. The moment which is the most dangerous to the honour and the safety of a British army is that in which they have won the place they have assaulted. While outside the walls, and linked together by the magic hand of discipline, they are heroes—but once they have forced themselves inside they become demons or lunatics—for it is difficult to determine which spirit predominates.

To see the two storming divisions assembled in the great square that night, mixed up in a confused mass, shooting at each other, and firing in at different doors and windows, without the shadow of a reason, was enough to drive any one, who was in possession of his senses, mad. The prisoners were formed in a line on one side of the square—unarmed, it is true—but, on my life, had they made a simultaneous rush forward, they might have made a second Bergen-op-Zoom of it—for so absolute was the sway of the demon of misrule, that half of our men, I verily believe, would have been panic-struck and thrown themselves into the arms of death, over the ramparts, to escape a danger that either did not exist or might have been easily avoided. After calling, and shouting, until I was hoarse in endeavouring to restore order, and when my voice was no longer audible, seeing a soldier raising his piece to fire at a window, I came across his shoulders with a musket-barrel which I had in my hand, and demanded, " What the devil, sir, are you firing at ?" to which he answered, " I don't know, sir ! I am firing because every body else is !"

The storming of a fortress was a new era to the British army of that day, and it is not to be wondered at if the officers were not fully alive to the responsibility which attaches to them on such an occasion—but on their conduct every thing hinges—by judgement and discretion men may be kept together—but once let them loose and they are no longer redeemable.

I have often lamented that speechifying was at such a discount in those days, for, excepting what was promulgated in Lord Wellington's orders, which were necessarily brief, the subordinates knew nothing of the past, present, or the future, until the glimpse of an English newspaper some months after served to enlighten their understandings; but there were every day occasions, in which the slightest hint from our superiors, as to the probable results, would have led to incalculable advantages, and in none more so than in the cases now quoted. So far from recommending caution, the chief of one of the storming divisions is grievously belied if he did not grant some special licenses for that particular occasion, though I am bound to say for him that he did all he could to repress them when he found the advantage taken.

Ciudad, being a remote frontier fortress, could boast of few persons of any note within its walls—our worthy friends of Horquera, (the

Alcaldé, with his family,) were probably the best, and he returned and resumed his official functions as soon as he found that the place had reverted to its legal owners—his house had been a princely one, but was, unfortunately, situated behind the great breach, and was blown to atoms—so that, for the time being, he was obliged to content himself with one more humble —though, if I may speak as I have felt, I should say not less comfortable, for I contrived to make it my home as often as I could find an excuse for so doing—and, as the old Proverb goes, " where there is a will there is a way," it was as often as I could.

One portion of the ceremony of Spanish hospitality was their awaking me about five in the morning to take a cup of chocolate, made so thick that a tea-spoon might stand in it, which, with a little crisp brown toast, was always administered by the fair hands of one of the damsels, and certes I never could bring myself to consider it an annoyance, however unusual it may seem in this cold land of ours.

CHAP. XI.

Very short, with a few anecdotes still shorter; but the principal actors thought the scenes long enough.

AFTER the fall of Ciudad Rodrigo, our battalion took possession for a time of Ituera, a pretty little village on the banks of the Azava.

It was a delightful coursing country, abounding in hares; and as the chase in those days afforded a double gratification—the one present, and the other in perspective, (the dinner hour,) it was always followed with much assiduity. The village, too, happened to be within a short ride of Ciudad, so that frequent visits to our friends formed an agreeable variety, and rendered our short sojourn there a season of real enjoyment.

I was much struck, on first entering Spain, in observing what appeared to be a gross absurdity

N

in their religious observances; for whenever one of those processions was heard approaching, the girls, no matter how they had been employed, immediately ran to the window, where, kneeling down, they continued repeating their *aves* until it had passed, when they jumped up again and were ready for any frolic or mischief.

Such was the effect produced inwardly by the outward passage of the *Hoste*, but it was not until I went to Ituera that I had an opportunity of witnessing the fatal results of a more familiar visit from those gentlemen bearing torches and dark lanterns, for they certainly seemed to me to put several souls to flight before they were duly prepared for it.

One happened to be the landlady of the house in which I was quartered, a woman about three score, and blind; but she was, nevertheless, as merry as a cricket, and used to amuse us over the fireside in the evening, while " twisting her rock and her wee pickle tow," in chaunting Malbrook and other ditties equally interesting, with a voice which at one time might have had a little music in it, but had then degenerated into the squeak of a penny trumpet.

In her last evening on earth, she had treated us with her usual serenade, and seemed as likely to live a dozen years longer as any one of the group around her; but on my return from a field-day next forenoon, I met the Padré, the sexton, and their usual accompaniments, marching out of the house to the tune of that *grave* air of theirs; and I saw that further question was needless, for the tears of the attendant damsels told me the tale of woe.

Her sudden departure was to me most unaccountable, nor could I ever obtain an explanation beyond that she was very aged; that they had sent for the Father to comfort her, and now she was happy in the keeping of their blessed Virgin.

There was much weeping and wailing for a day or two, and her grand-daughter, a tall thin lath of a girl, about eleven or twelve years of age, seemed the most distressed of the group. It so happened that a few days after, an order was promulgated authorising us to fill up our ranks

with Spanish recruits, to the extent of ten men
for each company, and I started off to some of
the neighbouring villages, where we were well-
known, in the hope of being able to pick up some
good ones.   On my return I was rather amused
to find that the damsel already mentioned, whom
I had left ten days before bathed in tears, was
already a blushing bride in the hands of a strap-
ping muleteer.

While on the subject of those Spanish recruits
I may here remark that we could not persuade
the countrymen to join us, and it was not until
we got to Madrid that we succeeded in procuring
the prescribed number for our battalion.   Those
we got, however, were a very inferior sample of
the Spaniard, and we therefore expected little
from them, but to their credit be it recorded,
they turned out admirably well—they were orderly and well-behaved in quarters, and thoroughly good in the field; and they never went
into action that they had not their full portion of
casualties.

There were fifty of them originally, and at the
close of the war, (about a year and a half after,)

I think there were about seventeen remaining, and there had not been a single desertion from among them. When we were leaving the country they received some months' gratuitous pay and were discharged, taking with them our best wishes, which they richly merited.

Lord Wellington during the whole of the war kept a pack of fox-hounds, and while they contributed not a little to the amusemeut of whatever portion of the army happened to be within reach of head-quarters, they were to his Lordship valuable in many ways; for while he enjoyed the chase as much as any, it gave him an opportunity of seeing and conversing with the officers of the different departments, and other individuals, without attracting the notice of the enemy's emissaries; and the pursuits of that manly exercise, too, gave him a better insight into the characters of the individuals under him, than he could possibly have acquired by years of acquaintance under ordinary circumstances.

It is not unusual to meet, in the society of the present day, some old Peninsular trump, with the rank very probably of a field officer, and with a face as polished, and its upper story as well furnished as the figure-head of his sword hilt, gravely asserting that all the merit which the Duke of Wellington has acquired from his victories was due to the troops ! And having plundered the Commander-in-Chief of his glory, and divided it among the followers, he, as an officer of those same followers, very complacently claims a field officer's allowance in the division of the spoil.

I would stake all I have in this world that no man ever heard such an opinion from the lips of a private soldier—I mean a thorough good service one—for the ideas of such men are beyond it ; and I have ever found that their proudest stories relate to the good or gallant deeds of those above them. It is impossible, therefore, to hear such absurdities advanced by one in the rank of an officer, without marvelling by what fortuitous piece of luck he, with the military capacity of a baggage animal, had contrived to hold his commission, for he must have been deeply indebted to the clemency of those above, and takes the usual method of that class of persons, to shew his sense thereof, by kicking down the ladder by which he ascended.

Our civil brethren in general are of necessity obliged to swallow a considerable portion of whatever we choose to place before them. But when they meet with such an one as I have described, they may safely calculate that whenever the items of his services can be collected, it will be found that his Majesty has had a hard bargain! For, knowing, as every one does, what the best ship's crew would be afloat in the wide world of waters without a master, they may, on the same principle, bear in mind that there can no more be an efficient army without a good general, than there can be an efficient general without a good army, for the one is part and parcel of the other—they cannot exist singly!

The touching on the foregoing subject naturally obliges me to wander from my narrative to indulge in a few professional observations, illustrative not only of war but of its instruments.

Those unaccustomed to warfare, are apt to imagine that a field of battle is a scene of confusion worse confounded, but that is a mistake, for, except on particular occasions, there is in general no noise or confusion any thing like what takes place on ordinary field days in England. I have often seen half the number of troops put to death, without half the bluster and confusion which takes place in a sham fight in the Phœnix-Park of Dublin.

The man who blusters at a field day is not the man who does it on the field of battle : on the contrary his thoughts there are generally too big for utterance, and he would gladly squeeze himself into a nutshell if he could. The man who makes a noise on the field of battle is generally a good one, but all rules have their exceptions, for I have seen one or two thorough good ones, who were blusterers in both situations ; but it nevertheless betrays a weakness in any officer who is habitually noisy about trifles, from the simple fact that when any thing of importance occurs to require an extraordinary exertion of lungs, nature cannot supply him with the powers requisite to make the soldiers understand that it is the consequence of an occurrence more serious, than the trifle he was in the habit of making a noise about.

In soldiering, as in every thing else, except Billingsgate and ballad singing, the cleverest things are done quietly.

At the storming of the heights of Bera, on the 8th of October, 1813, Colonel, now Sir John Colbourne, who commanded our second brigade, addressed his men before leading them up to the enemy's redoubt with, "Now, my lads, we'll just charge up to the edge of the ditch, and if we can't get in, we'll stand there and fire in their faces." They charged accordingly, the enemy fled from the works, and in following them up the mountain, Sir John, in rounding a hill, accompanied only by his brigade-major and a few riflemen, found that he had headed a retiring body of about 300 of the French, and whispering to his brigade-major to get as many men together as he could, he without hesitation rode boldly up to the enemy's commander, and demanded his sword ! The Frenchman surrendered it with the usual grace of his countrymen, requesting that the other would bear witness that he had conducted himself like a good and valiant soldier !   Sir John answered the appeal with an approving nod ; for it was no time to refuse bearing witness to the valour of 300 men, while they were in the act of surrendering to half a dozen.

If a body of troops is under fire, and so placed as to be unable to return it, the officer commanding should make it a rule to keep them constantly on the move, no matter if it is but two side steps to the right or one to the front, it always makes them believe they are doing something, and prevents the mind from brooding over a situation which is the most trying of any.

The coolness of an officer in action, if even shewn in trifles, goes a great way towards maintaining the steadiness of the men. At the battle of Waterloo, I heard Sir John Lambert call one of his commanding officers to order for repeating

his (the general's) word of command, reminding
him that when the regiments were in contiguous close columns, they ought to take it from
himself! As the brigade was under a terrific
fire at the time, the notice of such a trifling
breach of rule shewed, at all events, that the
gallant general was at home!

In the course of the five days' fighting which
took place near Bayonne, in December, 1813, a
singular change of fate, with its consequent interchange of civilities, took place between the
commanding officer of a French regiment and
one of ours; I forget whether it was the 4th or
9th, but I think it was one of the regiments of
that brigade—it had been posted amongst some
enclosures which left both its flanks at the
mercy of others.

The fighting at that place had been very
severe, with various success, and while the
regiment alluded to was hotly engaged in front,
a French corps succeeded in getting in their rear;
when the enemy's commandant advancing to
the English one, apologised for troubling him,

but begged to point out that he was surrounded, and must consider himself his prisoner! While the British colonel was listening to the mortifying intelligence, and glancing around to see if no hope of escape was left, he observed another body of English in the act of compassing the very corps by which he had been caught; and, returning the Frenchman's salute, begged his pardon for presuming to differ with him in opinion, but that he was labouring under a mistake, for he (the Frenchman) was, on the contrary, his prisoner, pointing in his turn to the movement that had taken place while they had been disputing the point. As the fact did not admit of a doubt, the Frenchman giving a shrug of the shoulders, and uttering a lament over the fickleness of the war-goddess, quietly surrendered.

CHAP. XII.

Shewing rough visitors receiving a rough reception. Some living and moving specimens thereof. Tailors not such fractions of humanity as is generally believed. Gentle visitors receiving a gentle reception, which ends by shewing that two shakes joined together sound more melodiously on the heart-strings than two hands which shake of their own accord.

Pass we on to Badajos—to that last, that direful, but glorious night—the 6th of April— " so fiercely fought, so terribly won, so dreadful in all its circumstances, that posterity can scarcely be expected to credit the tale."

Any one who has taken the trouble to read and digest what Napier has said in vindication of the measures adopted by Lord Wellington for the subjugation of those fortresses in the manner in which it was done, must feel satisfied that their propriety admits of no dispute. But as the want of time rendered it necessary to set the arts and sciences at defiance—and that, if carried at all, it must have been done with an extra sacrifice of human life, it will for ever remain a matter of opinion at what period of the siege the assault should have been made with the best prospect of success, and with the least probable loss—and such being the case it must be free to every writer to offer his own ideas.

Lord Wellington, as is well known, waited on each occasion for open breaches, and was each time successful—so far he did well, and they may do better who can. Colonel Lamarre would have attacked Badajos the first night of the siege with better hopes of success than on the last, as the garrison, he says, would have been less prepared, and the defences not so com plete. But I differ from him on both positions, for, depend upon it, that every garrison is excessively alive for the first few days after they have been invested. And as to defensive preparations, I have reason to think that few after ones of consequence took place, but those of counteracting the effects of our battering guns.

I am, nevertheless, one of those who would like to see the attempt made at an intermediate period. Breaches certainly serve the important end of distracting the attention of the garrison, and leading them to neglect other assailable points—though, whenever they have the opportunity of retrenching them, as at Badajos, they are undoubtedly the strongest parts of the works. I should therefore carry on the siege in the usual manner until about the time the batteries began to come into operation, and as it might then be fairly presumed that the garrison, by the regular order of proceedings, would be lulled into a notion of temporary security, I should feel monstrously inclined to try my luck. If it turned up trumps it might save valuable time and a thousand or two of valuable lives. If it failed, the loss would be in proportion; but it would neither lose time, nor compromise the result of the siege.

Colonel Jones, an able writer and an able fighter, in his particular department, would have had us do what his great guns ought to have done on that memorable night—namely, to have cleared away the defences on the top of the breach, which he affirms might have been done by the rush of a dense mass of troops. But had he been where I was he would have seen that there was no scarcity of rushes of dense masses of troops; but, independently of every other engine of destruction which human ingenuity could invent—they were each time met by a dense rush of balls, and it is the nature of man to bow before them. No dense mass of troops could reach the top of that breach.

Major (then Lieutenant) Johnston, of ours, who was peculiarly calculated for desperate enterprize, preceded the forlorn hope, in command of a party carrying ropes, prepared with nooses, to throw over the sword blades, as the most likely method of displacing, by dragging them down the breach; but he and his whole party were stricken down before one of them had got within throwing distance.

When an officer, as I have already mentioned, with a presentiment of death upon him, re-signed a safe duty to take a desperate one—when my own servant, rather than remain behind, gave up his situation and took his place in the ranks—when another man of ours (resolved to win or to die, thrust himself beneath the chained sword blades, and there suffered the enemy to dash his brains out with the ends of their muskets—these, I say, out of as many thousand instances of the kind which may be furnished, will shew that there was no want of daring leaders or desperate followers.

The defences on the tops of the breaches ought to have been cleared away by our batteries before the assault commenced. But failing that, I cannot see why a couple of six-pounders (or half a dozen) might not have been run up

along with the storming party, to the crest of
the glacis. Our battalion took post there, and
lay about ten minutes unknown to the enemy,
and had a few guns been sent along with us,
I am confident that we could have taken them
up with equal silence, and had them pointed at
the right place—when, at the time that the
storming party commenced operations, a single
discharge from each, at that range of a few
yards, would not only have disturbed the economy of the sword blades and sand-bags, but
astonished the wigs of those behind them. As it
was, however, when I visited the breaches next
morning, instead of seeing the ruin of a place
just carried by storm, the whole presented the
order and regularity of one freshly prepared to
meet it—not a sword blade deranged, nor a
sand-bag removed !

The advance of the fourth division had been
delayed by some accident, and the head of their
column did not reach the ditch until our first
attack had been repulsed, and when considerable confusion consequently prevailed.

The seventh Fusileers came gallantly on, headed by Major ——, who, though a very little man, shouted with the lungs of a giant, for the way to be cleared, to " let the royal Fusileers advance!" Several of our officers assisted him in such a laudable undertaking; but, in the mean time, a musket-ball found its way into some sensitive part, and sent the gallant major trundling heels over head among the loose stones, shouting to a less heroic tune—while his distinguished corps went determinedly on, but with no better success than those who had just preceded them, for the thing was not to be done.

After we had withdrawn from the ditch and reformed the division for a renewal of the attack, (it must have been then about two or three o'clock in the morning,) some of those on the look-out brought us information that the enemy were leaving the breaches, and our battalion was instantly moved forward to take possession.

We stole down into the ditch with the same silence which marked our first advauce—an occasional explosion or a discharge of musketry continued to be heard in distant parts of the works; but in the awful charnel pit we were then traversing to reach the foot of the breach, the only sounds that disturbed the night were the moans of the dying, with an occasional screech from others suffering under acute agony; while a third class lying there disabled, and alive to passing events, on hearing the movement of troops, (though too dark to distinguish them,) began proclaiming their names and regiments, and appealing to individual officers and soldiers of the different corps, on whose friendly aid they seemed to feel that they could rely if they happened to be within hearing.

It was a heart-rending moment to be obliged to leave such appeals unheeded; but, though the fate of those around might have been ours the next instant, our common weal, our honour, and our country's, alike demanded that every thing should be sacrificed to secure the prize which was now within our grasp; and our onward movement was therefore continued into the breach with measured tread and stern silence, leaving the unfortunate sufferers to doubt whether the stone walls around had not been their only listeners.

Once established within the walls we felt satisfied that the town was ours—and, profiting by his experience at Ciudad, our commandant (Colonel Cameron) took the necessary measures to keep his battalion together, so long as the safety of the place could in any way be compromised—for, knowing the barbarous license which soldiers employed in that desperate service claim, and which they will not be denied, he addressed them, and promised that they should have the same indulgence as others, and that he should not insist upon keeping them together longer than was absolutely necessary; but he assured them that if any man quitted the ranks until he gave permission he would cause him to be put to death on the spot. That had the desired effect until between nine and ten o'clock in the morning, when, seeing that the whole of the late garrison had been secured and marched off to Elvas, he again addressed his battalion, and thanked them for their conduct throughout : he concluded with, " Now, my men, you may fall out and enjoy yourselves for the remainder of the day, but I shall expect to see you all in camp at the usual roll-call in the evening !"

When the evening came, however, in place of the usual tattoo report of all present, it was all absent, and it could have been wished that the irregularities had ended with that evening's report.

As soon as a glimpse of day-light permitted I went to take a look at the breach, and there saw a solitary figure, with a drawn sword, stalking over the ruins and the slain, which, in the grey dawn of morning, appeared to my astonished eyes like a headless trunk, and concluded that it was the ghost of one of the departed come in ·search of its earthly remains. I cautiously approached to take a nearer survey, when I found that it was Captain M'Nair, of the 52d, with his head wrapped in a red handkerchief.

He told me that he was looking for his cap and his scabbard, both of which had parted company from him in the storm, about that particular spot; but his search proved a forlorn hope. I congratulated him that his head had not gone in the cap, as had been the case with but too many of our mutual companions on that fatal night.

When our regiment had reformed after the assault we found a melancholy list of absent officers, ten of whom were doomed never to see it more, and it was not until our return to the camp that we learnt the fate of all.

The wounded had found their way or been removed to their own tents—the fallen filled a glorious grave on the spot where they fell.

The first tent that I entered was Johnston's, with his shattered arm bandaged; he was lying on his boat-cloak fast asleep; and, coupling his appearance with the recollection of the daring duty he had been called on to perform but a few hours before, in front of the forlorn hope, I

thought that I had never set my eyes on a no-
bler picture of a soldier. His whole appearance,
even in sleep, shewed exactly as it had been in
the execution of that duty; his splendid figure
was so disposed that it seemed as if he was
taking the first step on the breach—his eyebrows
were elevated—his nostrils still distended—and,
altogether, he looked as if he would clutch the
castle in his remaining hand. No one could
have seen him at that moment without saying,
" there lies a hero!"

Of the doomed, who still survived, was poor
Donald Mac Pherson, a gigantic highlander of
about six feet and a half, as good a soul as ever
lived; in peace a lamb—in war a lion. Donald
feared for nothing either in this world or the
next; he had been true to man and true to his
God, and he looked his last hour in the face
like a soldier and a Christian!

Donald's final departure from this life shewed
him a worthy specimen of his country, and his
methodical arrangements, while they prove what
I have stated, may, at the same time, serve as

as a model for Joe Hume himself, when he comes to cast up his last earthly accounts.

Donald had but an old mare and a portmanteau, with its contents, worth about £15, to leave behind him. He took a double inventory of the latter, sending one to the regiment by post, and giving the other in charge of his servant—and paying the said worthy his wages up to the probable day of his death; he gave him a conditional order on the paymaster for whatever more might be his due should he survive beyond his time—and, if ever man did, he certainly quitted this world with a clear conscience.

Poor Donald! peace be to thy manes, for thou wert one whom memory loves to dwell on!

It is curious to remark the fatality which attends individual officers in warfare. In our regiment there were many fine young men who joined us, and fell in their first encounter with the enemy; but, amongst the old standing dishes, there were some who never, by any chance got hit, while others, again, never went into action without.

O

At the close of the war, when we returned to England, if our battalion did not shew symptoms of its being a well-shot corps, it is very odd : nor was it to be wondered at if the camp-colours were not covered with that precision, nor the salute given with the grace usually expected from a reviewed body, when I furnish the following account of the officers commanding companies on the day of inspection, viz.

Beckwith with a cork-leg—Pemberton and Manners with a shot each in the knee, making them as stiff as the other's tree one—Loftus Gray with a gash in the lip, and minus a portion of one heel, which made him march to the tune of dot and go one—Smith with a shot in the ankle—Eeles minus a thumb—Johnston, in addition to other shot holes, a stiff elbow, which deprived him of the power of disturbing his friends as a scratcher of Scotch reels upon the violin—Percival with a shot through his lungs. Hope with a grape-shot lacerated leg—and George Simmons with his riddled body held together by a pair of stays, for his was no holyday waist, which

naturally required such an appendage lest the
burst of a sigh should snap it asunder; but
one that appertained to a figure framed in nature's fittest mould to "brave the battle and
the breeze!"

I know not to what particular circumstances
British tailors were in the first instance indebted, for ranking them so low in the scale
of humanity, but, as far as my knowledge ex-
tends, there never was a more traduced race.
Those of our regiment I know were among
the best soldiers in it, and more frequently hit
than any, very much to our mortification; for
the very limited allowance of an officer's campaigning baggage left him almost constantly at
their mercy for the decoration of his outward
man; but as the musket-balls shewed no mercy
to them, we could not of course expect them to
extend it to us.

Our master-man having at this time got his
third shot, we deemed it high time to place him
on the shelf, by confining his operations in the
field, to the baggage guard. So long as we

could preserve him in a condition to wield the scissors, we luckily discovered that there were minor thimble-plyers ready to rally round him, for we should otherwise have been driven sometimes to the extraordinary necessity of invading the nether garments of the ladies !

The last night at Badajos had been to the belligerents such as few had ever seen—the next, to its devoted inhabitants, was such as none would ever wish to see again, for there was no sanctuary within its walls.

I was conversing with a friend the day after, at the door of his tent, when we observed two ladies coming from the city, who made directly towards us; they seemed both young, and when they came near, the elder of the two threw back her *mantilla* to address us, shewing a remarkably handsome figure, with fine features, but her sallow, sunburnt, and careworn, though still youthful countenance, shewed that in her, " The time for tender thoughts and soft endearments had fled away and gone."

She at once addressed us in that confident

heroic manner so characteristic of the high bred
Spanish maiden, told us who they were, the last
of an ancient and honourable house, and referred
to an officer high in rank in our army, who had
been quartered there in the days of her pros-
perity, for the truth of her tale.

Her husband she said was a Spanish officer
in a distant part of the kingdom; he might or
he might not still be living. But yesterday, she
and this her young sister were able to live in
affluence and in a handsome house—to day,
they knew not where to lay their heads—where
to get a change of raiment or a morsel of bread.
Her house, she said, was a wreck, and to shew
the indignities to which they had been subjected,
she pointed to where the blood was still trickling
down their necks, caused by the wrenching of
their earrings through the flesh, by the hands of
worse than savages who would not take the
trouble to unclasp them!

For herself, she said, she cared not; but for
the agitated, and almost unconscious maiden by
her side, whom she had but lately received over

from the hands of her conventual instructresses, she was in despair, and knew not what to do; and that in the rapine and ruin which was at that moment desolating the city, she saw no security for her but the seemingly indelicate one she had adopted, of coming to the camp and throwing themselves upon the protection of any British officer who would afford it; and so great, she said, was her faith in our national character, that she knew the appeal would not be made in vain, nor the confidence abused. Nor was it made in vain! nor could it be abused, for she stood by the side of an angel!—A being more transcendantly lovely I had never before seen—one more amiable, I have never yet known!

Fourteen summers had not yet passed over her youthful countenance, which was of a delicate freshness, more English than Spanish— her face though not perhaps rigidly beautiful, was nevertheless so remarkably handsome, and so irresistibly attractive, surmounting a figure cast in nature's fairest mould, that to look at her was to love her—and I did love her; but I never told my love, and in the meantime another, and a more impudent fellow stepped in and won her ! but yet I was happy—for in him she found such a one as her loveliness and her misfortunes claimed—a man of honour, and a husband in every way worthy of her!

That a being so young, so lovely, so interesting, just emancipated from the gloom of a convent, unknowing of the world and to the world unknown, should thus have been wrecked on a sea of troubles, and thrown on the mercy of strangers under circumstances so dreadful, so uncontrollable, and not to have sunk to rise no more, must be the wonder of every one. Yet from the moment she was thrown on her own resources, her star was in the ascendant.

Guided by a just sense of rectitude, an innate purity of mind, a singleness of purpose which defied malice, and a soul that soared above circumstances, she became alike the adored of the camp and of the drawing-room, and eventually the admired associate of princes. She yet lives, in the affections of her gallant husband in an elevated situation in life, a pattern to her sex, and the every body's *beau ideal* of what a wife should be.

My reader will perhaps bear with me on this subject yet a little longer.

Thrown upon each other's acquaintance in a manner so interesting, it is not to be wondered at that she and I conceived a friendship for each other, which has proved as lasting as our lives— a friendship which was cemented by after circumstances so singularly romantic, that imagination may scarcely picture them! The friendship of man is one thing—the friendship of woman another; and those only who have been on the theatre of fierce warfare, and knowing that such a being was on the spot, watching with earnest and unceasing solicitude over his safety, alike with those most dear to her, can fully appreciate the additional value which it gives to one's existence.

About a year after we became acquainted, I remember that our battalion was one day moving down to battle, and had occasion to pass by the lone country-house in which she had been lodged.

The situation was so near to the outposts, and a battle certain, I concluded that she must ere then have been removed to a place of greater security, and, big with the thought of coming events, I scarcely even looked at it as we rolled along, but just as I had passed the door, I found my hand suddenly grasped in her's—she gave it a gentle pressure, and without uttering a word had rushed back into the house again, almost before I could see to whom I was indebted for a kindness so unexpected and so gratifying.

My mind had the moment before been sternly occupied in calculating the difference which it makes in a man's future prospects—his killing or being killed, when " a change at once came o'er the spirit of the dream," and throughout the remainder of that long and trying day, I felt a lightness of heart and buoyancy of spirit which, in such a situation, was no less new than delightful.

I never, until then, felt so forcibly the beautiful description of Fitz James's expression of feeling, after his leave-taking of Helen under somewhat similar circumstances :—

> " And after oft the knight would say,
> That not when prize of festal day,
> Was dealt him by the brightest fair
> That e'er wore jewel in her hair,
> So highly did his bosom swell,
> As at that simple, mute, farewell."

CHAP. XIII.

Specimens of target-practice, in which markers may become marked men.—A grave anecdote, shewing how " some men have honours thrust upon them."—A line drawn between man and beast.—Lines drawn between regiments, and shewing how credit may not be gained by losing what they are made of.—Aristocratic.—Dedicatic.—Dissertation on advanced guards, and desertion of knapsacks, shewing that " the greater haste the worse speed."

WITH discipline restored, Badajos secured, and the French relieving army gone to the right about, we found ourselves once more transferred to the North.

Marmont had, during our absence, thrown away much valuable time in cutting some unmeaning vagaries before the Portuguese militia, which, happily for us, he might have spent more profitably; and now that we approached him, he fell back upon Salamanca, leaving us to take quiet possession of our former cantonments.

Lord Wellington had thus, by a foresight almost superhuman, and by a rapidity of execution equal to the conception, succeeded in snatching the two frontier fortresses out of the enemy's hands in the face of their superior armies, it gave him a double set of keys for the security of rescued Portugal, and left his victorious army free and unfettered for the field.

We had been on the watch long enough, with the enemy before, beside, and around us; but it had now become their turn to look out for squalls, and by and bye they caught it—but in the meanwhile we were allowed to have some respite after the extraordinary fatigues of the past.

Spring had by that time furnished the face of nature with her annual suit of regimentals, (I wish it had done as much for us,) our pretty little village stood basking in the sunshine of the plain, while the surrounding forest courted the lovers of solitude to repose within its shady bosom. There the nightingale and the bee-bird made love to their mates—and there too the wolf made love to his meat, for which he preferred the hind-quarter of a living horse, but failing that, he did not despise a slice from a mule or a donkey.

Nature seemed to have intended that region as the abode of rural tranquillity, but man had doomed it otherwise. The white tent rearing its fiery top among the green leaves of the forest—the war-steed careering on the plains—the voice of the trumpet for the bleat of the lamb—and the sharp clang of the rifle with its thousand echoes reverberating from the rocks at target-practice, were none of them in keeping with the scene; so that the nightingale was fain to hush its melody, and the wolf his howl, until a change of circumstances should restore him to his former sinecure of head ranger.

The actors on that busy scene too continued to be wild and reckless as their occupation, their lives had been so long in perpetual jeopardy that they now held them of very little value. A rifleman one day in marking the target, went behind to fix it more steadily; another, who did not observe him go there, sent a ball through, which must have passed within a hair's breadth of the marker, but the only notice he took was to poke his head from behind, and thundering out, " Hilloah there, d—— your eyes, do you mean to shoot us ?" went on with his work as if it had been nothing.

Whilst on the subject of rifle-shooting, and thinking of the late Indian exhibition of its nicety on the London stage, it reminds me that the late Colonel Wade, and one of the privates of our second battalion, were in the habit of holding the target for each other at the distance of 200 yards.

I cannot think of those days without reflecting on the mutability of human life, and the chances and changes which man is heir to. For, to think that I, who had so many years been the sleeping and waking companion of dead men's bones, and not only accustomed to hold them valueless, but often to curse the chance " which brought them between the wind and my nobility ;" I say that, under such circumstances, to think I should e'er have stood the chance of dying the death of a body snatcher, is to me astonishing, and would shew, even without any scriptural authority, " that in the midst of life we are in death," for so it was.

Some years after, I was on my way from Ireland to Scotland, when I was taken seriously ill at Belfast. After being confined to bed several days in a hotel there, and not getting better, I became anxious to reach home, and had myself conveyed on board a steam-boat which was on the point of sailing.

I had been but a few minutes in bed when I heard a confused noise about the boat; but I was in a low, listless mood, dead to every thing but a feeling of supreme misery, until my cabin-door was opened, and the ugly faces of several legal understrappers protruded themselves, and began to reconnoitre me with a strong sinister expression; I was dead even to that, but when they at length explained, that in searching the luggage of the passengers, they had found a defunct gentleman in one of the boxes, and as

he belonged to nobody out of bed, he must naturally be the property of the only one in it, viz.
myself! a very reasonable inference, at which I
found it high time to stir myself, the more par-
cularly as the intimation was accompanied by
an invitation to visit the police-office.

My unshaved countenance worn down to a
most cadaverous hue with several days intense
suffering, was but ill calculated to bear me out
in assertions to the contrary, but having some
documentary evidence to shew who I was, and
seeing too that I was really the invalid which
they thought I had only affected, they went
away quite satisfied. Not so, however, the mob
without, who insisted on being allowed to judge
for themselves, so that the officers were obliged
to return and beg of me to shew myself at the
cabin window to pacify them.

There is no doubt but I must at that time,
have borne a much stronger resemblance to the
gentleman in the box, than to the gentleman
proprietor; but to shew the justice and dis-
crimination of mobites, I had no sooner

exhibited my countenance such as it was, than half of them shouted that they knew me to be the man, and demanded that I should be handed over to them; and had there not been some of the family of the hotel fortunately on board seeing their friends off, who vouched for my authenticity, and for my having been in bed in their house ever since I came to town, there is little doubt but they would have made a *subject* of me.

Returning from this grave anecdote to the seat of war, I pass on to the assembling of the army in front of Ciudad Rodrigo preparatory to the advance upon Salamanca.

Our last assemblage on the same spot was to visit the walls of that fortress with the thunder of our artillery, and having, by the force of such persuasive arguments, succeeded in converting them into friends, in whom, with confidence, we might rely in the hour of need, we were now about to bid them and our peasant associates an adieu, with a fervent wish on our part that it might be a final one, while with joy

we looked forward to the brightening prospect
which seemed to promise us an opportunity of
diving a little deeper into their land of romance
than we had yet done.

Division after division of our iron framed warriors successively arrived, and took possession
of the rugged banks of the Agueda, in gallant
array and in gayer shape than formerly, for in
our first campaigns the canopy of heaven had
been our only covering, and our walking on two
legs, clothed in rags, the only distinction between us and the wild beast of the forest—
whereas we were now indulged in the before
unheard of luxury of a tent—three being allowed to the soldiers of each company, and one
to the officers.

There is nothing on earth so splendid—nothing so amusing to a military soul as this assembling of an army for active service—to see
fifty thousand men all actuated by one common spirit of enterprize, and the cause their
country's! And to see the manner, too, in
which it acts on the national characters enlisted

in it—the grave-looking, but merry-hearted Englishman—the canny, cautious, and calculating Scotchman, and the devil-may-care *nonchalance* of the Irish.

I should always prefer to serve in a mixed corps, but I love to see a national one—for while the natives of the three amalgamate well, and make, generally speaking, the most steady, there is nevertheless an *esprit* about a national one which cannot fail to please.

Nothing occasions so much controversy in civil life as the comparative merits of those same corps—the Scotchman claiming every victory in behalf of his countrymen, and the Irishman being no less voracious—so that the unfortunate English regiments, who furnish more food for powder than both put together, are thus left to fight and die unhonoured.

Those who know no better naturally enough award the greatest glory to the greatest sufferers; but that is no true criterion—for great loss in battle, in place of being a proof of superior valour and discipline, is not unfrequently occasioned by a want of the latter essential.

The proudest trophy which the commanding officer of a regiment can ever acquire is the credit of having done a brilliant deed with little loss—and although there are many instances in which they may justly boast of such misfortunes —witness the fifty-seventh at Albuera, the twenty-seventh at Waterloo, and a hundred similar cases, in which they nearly all perished on the spot they were ordered to defend, yet I am of opinion that if the sentiments of old service officers could be gathered, it would be found among a majority, that their proudest regimental days were not those on which they had suffered most.

National regiments have perhaps a greater *esprit de corps* generally than the majority of mixed ones, but in action they are more apt to be carried away by some sudden burst of undisciplined valour, as Napier would have it, to the great danger of themselves and others.

An Irishman, after the battle of Vimiera, in writing home to his friends, said, " We charged them over fifteen leagues of country, we never waited for the word of command, for we were all Irish!" And I think I could furnish a Highland anecdote or two of a similar tendency.

In the present day, the crack national regiments, officered as they are with their share of the *elite* of their country's youth, are not to be surpassed—but in war time I have never considered a crack national regiment equal to a crack mixed one.

The Irishman seems sworn never to drink water when he can get whiskey, unless he likes it better—the Scotchman, for a soldier, sometimes shews too much of the lawyer—the Englishman, too, has his besetting sin—but by mixing the three in due proportions, the evils are found to counteract each other. As regards personal bravery there is not a choice among them —and for the making of a perfect regiment I should therefore prescribe one-half English, and of Irish and Scotch a quarter each. Yet, as I said before, I love to see a national corps, and hope never to see a British army without them.

With regard to officers, I think I mentioned before that in war we had but a slender sprinkling of the aristocracy among us. The reason I consider a very sensible one, for whatever may be the sins with which they have, at different times, been charged, the want of pluck has never been reckoned among the number. But as there never was any scarcity of officers for the field, and consequently their country did not demand the sacrifice—they may very conscientiously stand acquitted for not going abroad, to fight and be starved, when they could live at home in peace and plenty.

I have often lamented however that a greater number had not been induced to try their fortunes on the tented field, for I have ever found that their presence and example tended to correct many existing evils. How it should have happened I leave to others, but I have rarely known one who was not beloved by those under him. They were not better officers, nor were they better or braver men than the soldiers of fortune,* with which they were mingled ; but there was a degree of refinement in all their actions, even in mischief, which commanded the respect of the soldiers, while those who had been framed in rougher moulds, and left unpolished, were sometimes obliged to have recourse to harsh measures to enforce it. The example was therefore invaluable for its tendency to shew that habitual severity was not a necessary ingredient in the art of governing—and however individuals may affect to despise and condemn the higher orders, it is often because they feel that they sink in the comparison, and thus it is that they will ever have their cringers and imitators even among their abusers.

I have, without permission, taken the liberty of dedicating this volume to one of their number—not because he is one of them, but that he is what I have found him—a nobleman ! I dedicate it to him, because, though personally

* Meaning soldiers of no fortune.

unacquainted, I knew and admired him in war, as one of the most able and splendid assistants of the illustrious chief with whom he served— and, " though poor the offering be," I dedicate it to him in gratitude, that with no other recommendation than my public services, I have ever since the war experienced at his hands a degree of consideration and kindness which none but a great and a good man could have known how to offer.

It may appear to my reader that I have no small share of personal vanity to gratify in making this announcement, and I own it. I am proud that I should have been thought deserving of his lordship's notice, but I am still prouder that it is in my power to give myself as an example that men of rank in office are not all of them the heartless beings which many try to make them appear.

With the army assembled, and the baggage laden on a fine May morning, I shall place every infantry man on his legs, the dragoon in his saddle, and the followers on their donkeys,

starting the whole cavalcade off on the high
road to Salamanca, which, being a very unin-
teresting one, and without a shot to enliven the
several days' march, I shall take advantage of
the opportunity it affords to treat my young
military readers to a dissertation on advanced
guards—for we have been so long at peace that
the customs of war in the like cases are liable
to be forgotten, unless rubbed into existence
from time to time by some such old foggy as I
am, and for which posterity can never feel sufficiently thankful, as to see our army taking the
field with the advanced guard on a plain, prescribed by the book of regulations, would bring
every old soldier to what I for one am not prepared for—a premature end; as however well the
said advanced guard may be calculated to find
birds' nests in a barrack square or on a common
parade, in the field it would worry an army to death.

In the first place, if a plain is an honest plain,
it requires no advanced guard, for a man's eyes
are not worth preserving if they cannot help him

P

to see three or four miles all round about—but there is no such thing as a plain any where. Look at the plains of Salamanca, where you may fancy that you see fifty miles straight on end without so much as a wart on the face of nature, as big as a mole hill; yet within every league or two you find yourself descending into a ravine a couple of miles deep, taking half a day to regain the plain on the opposite side, within a couple of stones' throw of where you were.

In place of harassing the men with perpetual flank patroles, blistering their feet over the loose stones with shoes full of sand, and expending their valuable wind, which is so much wanted towards the end of the day, in scrambling over uneven ground, let me recommend the advanced guard to confine itself to the high road until patrolling becomes necessary, which, in a forest, will be from the time they enter until they leave it, unless they can trust to the information that the enemy are otherwise engaged. And in the open country every officer commanding a regiment, troop, or company, who has got half a military eye in his head, will readily see when it is advisable to send a patrole to examine any particular ground ; and in so doing his best guide is to remember the amount of the force which he covers ; for while he knows that the numbers necessary to surprize an army of fifty thousand men cannot be conveniently crammed within the compass of a nutshell, he must, on the other hand, remember that there are few countries which do not afford an ambuscade for five or ten thousand—*ergo*, if there be any truth in Cocker, the man covering five thousand men must look exactly ten times sharper than the man who covers fifty thousand.

With an army of rough and ready materials such as ours had now become, the usual precautions were scarcely necessary, except in the immediate vicinity of the foe, for they had by this time discovered that it was more easy to find than to get rid of us ; but they ought, nevertheless, to be strictly observed at all times, unless there are good and sufficient reasons why they need not.

In an open country a few squadrons of dragoons shoved well to the front will procure every necessary information; but, in a close country, I hold the following to be the best advanced guard.

1st. A subaltern with twelve hussars, throwing two of them a hundred yards in front, and four at fifty.

2d. A section of riflemen or light infantry at fifty yards.

3d. The other three sections of the company at fifty yards.

4th. Four companies of light infantry at a hundred yards, with communicating files, and followed closely by two pieces of horse artillery, and a squadron of dragoons.

On falling in with the enemy, the advanced videttes will fire off their carabines to announce it, and if their opponents fall back they will continue their onward movement. If they do not, the intermediate four will join them, and try the result of a shot each; when, if the enemy still remain, it shews that they decline taking a civil hint, which, if they are infantry, they assuredly will; and dispositions must be made accordingly. While the remaining hussars are therefore dispatched to watch the flanks, the leading section of infantry will advance in skirmishing order, and take possession of the most favourable ground near the advanced videttes. The other three sections will close up to within fifty yards, one of them, if necessary, to join the advanced one, but a subdivision must remain in reserve. The guns will remain on the road, and the dragoons and infantry composing the main body of the advanced guard will be formed on the flanks, in such manner as the ground will admit, so as to be best ready for either attack or defence; and in that disposition they will wait further orders, presuming that the officer commanding the division will not be a hundred miles off.

The foregoing applies more particularly to the following of an enemy whom you have not lately

thrashed, whereas, if following a beaten one, he
ought never to be allowed a moment's respite so
long as you have force enough of any kind up
to shove him along. He ought to be bullied
every inch of the way with dragoons and horse
artillery, and the infantry brought to bear as
often as possible.

However much additional celerity of movement on the part of the latter force may be
desirable, I must impress upon the minds of all
future comptrollers of knapsacks, that on no
consideration should an infantry man ever be
parted from his pack. He will not move a bit
faster without than he does with it, nor do I
think he can do a yard further in a day's walking; they become so accustomed to the pace,
and so inured to the load, that it makes little
difference to them whether it is on or off,*

* Lightly however as they felt the load at the time, it was
one that told fearfully on the constitution, and I have seen
many men discharged in consequence, as being worn out, at
thirty-five years of age.

while the leaving of them behind leads, at all times, to serious loss, and to still more serious inconvenience.

The rifles during the war were frequently, as an indulgence, made to fight without them, but on every occasion it proved a sacrifice, and a great one. For although they were carried for us by the dragoons, who followed after, yet as our skirmishing service took us off the road, the kit of every man who got wounded was sure to be lost, for while he was lying kicking on his back in the middle of a field, or behind a stone wall, impatiently waiting for assistance, his knapsack had passed on to the front, and was never heard of more, (for every one has quite enough to do to take care of his own affairs on those occasions,) and the poor fellow was thus deprived of his comforts at a time when they were most needed. A dragoon, too, carrying several of them would sometimes get hit, and he of course pitched them all to the devil, while he took care of himself, and the unfortunate owners after their hard day's fighting were compelled to sleep in the open air for that and many succeeding nights, without the use of their blankets or necessaries. On one occasion I remember that they were left on the ground, and the battle rolled four miles beyond them, so that when it was over, and every one had already done enough, the soldiers were either obliged to go without, or to add eight or ten miles walk to a harassing day's work.

The secretary at war eventually came in for his share of the trouble attendant on those movements, for many were the claims for compensation which poured in upon the War-Office in after years, by the poor fellows who had bled and lost their all upon those occasions, nor do I know whether they have ever yet been set at rest.

So much for advanced guards and people in a hurry, and as I happen to have a little leisure time and a vacant leaf or two to fill up, I shall employ it in taking a shot at field fortification; and in so doing, be it remarked, that I leave science in those matters to the scientific, for I am but a practical soldier.

The French shewed themselves regular moles at field work, for they had no sooner taken post on a fresh position, than they were to be seen stirring up the ground in all directions. With us it was different. I have always understood that Lord Wellington had a dislike to them, and would rather receive his enemy in the open field than from behind a bank of mud. How far it was so I know not; but the report seemed to be verified by circumstances, for he rarely ever put us to the trouble of throwing up either redoubts or breast works, except at particular outposts, where they were likely to be useful. At Fuentes indeed he caused some holes to be dug on the right of the line, in which the enemy's cavalry might have comfortably broken their necks without hurting themselves much ; but I do not recollect our ever disturbing the ground any where else—leaving the lines of Torres Vedras out of the question, as containing works of a different order.

If time and circumstances permitted common field works to be so constructed as to prevent an enemy from scrambling up the walls, they would indeed be a set of valuable pictures in the face of a position; but as with mud alone they never can, I, for one, hold them to be worse than nothing, and would rather go against one of them, than against the same number of men in the open field.

It is true that in such a place they will suffer less in the first instance, but if they do not re-pulse their assailants or make a speedy retreat, they are sure to be all netted in the long run, and the consequence is, that one rarely sees a work of that kind well defended, for while its garrison is always prepared for a start, its fire is not so destructive as from the same number of men in the field, for in the field they will do their duty, but in the redoubt they will not, and half of their heads will be well sheltered under the ramparts, while they send the shot off at ran-dom. I know the fellows well, and it is only to swarm a body of light troops against the nearest angle, to get into the ditch as quickly as pos-sible, to unkennel any garrison of that kind very

cleverly, unless there be other obstacles than
their bayonets to contend against.

From field works I return to our work in the
field, to state that after several days march
under a broiling hot sun, and on roads of
scorching dust, which makes good stiff broth in
winter, we found ourselves on the banks of the
Tormes, near the end of the bridge of Salamanca; but as the gatekeeper there required
change for twenty-four pound shot, and we had
none at the moment to give him, we were obliged to take to the stream.

I know not what sort of toes the Pope keeps
for his friends to kiss, but I know that after a
week's marching in summer I would not kiss
those of the army for a trifle ; however, I suppose that walking feet and kissing ones wear
quite different pairs of shoes. The fording of
the clear broad waters of the Tormes at all
events proved a luxury in various ways, and
considerably refreshed by that part of the ceremony, we found ourselves shortly after in the
heart of that classical city, where the first

classics which we were called upon to study, were those of three forts, of a class of their own, which was well calculated to keep their neighbours in a constant supply of hot water. They were not field works such as I have been treating of in the last few pages, but town ones, with walls steep enough and ditches deep enough to hold the army, if packed like herrings. For ourselves we passed on to the front, leaving the seventh division to deal with them ; and a hard bargain they drove for a time, though they finally brought them to terms.

I rode in from the outposts several times to visit them during the siege, and on one occasion finding an officer, stationed in a tower, overlooking the works and acting under rather particular orders, it reminded me of an anecdote that occurred with us in the early part of the war. One of our majors had posted a subaltern with a party of riflemen in the tower of a church, and as the place was an important one, he ordered the officer, in the event of an attack, never to quit the place alive ! In the course

of the evening the commanding officer went to
visit the picquet, and after satisfying himself on
different points, he demanded of Lieut. ———
what dispositions he had made for retreat in the
event of his post being forced?—To which the
other replied, " None." " None, Sir," said the
commanding officer, " then let me tell you that
you have neglected an important part of your
duty." " I beg your pardon," returned the
officer, " but my orders are never to quit this
spot alive, and therefore no arrangements for
retreat can be necessary!" It may be needless
to add that a discretionary power was then extended to him.

In a midnight visit which I paid to the same
place in company with a staff friend, while the
batteries were in full operation, we were admiring the splendour of the scene, the crash of
the artillery, and the effect of the light and
shade on the ruins around, caused by the perpetual flashes from the guns and fire-balls,
when it recalled to his remembrance the siege
of Copenhagen, where he described a similar

scene which was enacted, but in a position so much more interesting.

The burying-grounds in the neighbourhood of that capital, were generally very tastefully laid out like shrubberies with beds of flowers, appropriate trees, &c., and intersected by winding gravel-walks, neatly bordered with box. One of the prettiest of these cemeteries was that at the Lecton suburb, in which there was a profusion of white marble statues of men and women—many of them in loose flowing drapery, and also of various quadrupeds, erected in commemoration or in illustration of the habits and virtues of the dead. These statues were generally overshadowed by cypress and other *lugubrious* trees.

Closely adjoining this beautiful cemetery, two heavy batteries were erected, one of ten-inch mortars, and the other of twenty-four pound battering guns.

In passing alone through this receptacle of the dead, about the hour of midnight, the rapid flashes of the artillery seemed to call all these statues, men, women, and beasts, with all their dismal accompaniments, into a momentary and ghastly existence—and the immediate succession of the deep gloom of midnight produced an effect which, had it been visible to a congregation of Scotch nurses, would in their hands have thrown all the goblin tales of their ancestors into the shade, and generations of bairns yet unborn would have had to shudder at the midnight view of a church-yard.

Even among the stern hearts to whose view alone it was open, the spectacle was calculated to excite very interesting reflections. The crash of the artillery on both sides was enough to have awakened the dead, then came the round shot with its wholesale sweep, tearing up the ornamental trees and dashing statues into a thousand pieces,—next came the bursting shell sending its fragments chattering among the tombs and defacing everything it came in contact with. These, all these came from the Danes themselves, and who knew but the hand that levelled the gun which destroyed that statue was not the same which had erected it to the memory of a beloved wife? Who knew but that the evergreens which had just been torn by a shot from a new-made grave, were planted there over the remains of an angelic daughter, and watered by the tears of the man who fired it? and who knew but that that exquisitely chiseled marble figure, which had its nose and eye defaced by a bursting shell, was not placed there to commemorate the decease of a beauteous and adored sweetheart, and valued more than existence by him who had caused its destruction!

Ah me! war, war! that

> " Snatching from the hand
> Of Time, the scythe of ruin, sits aloft,
> Or stalks in dreadful majesty abroad."

I know not what sort of place Salamanca was on ordinary occasions, but at that time it was remarkably stupid. The inhabitants were yet too much at the mercy of circumstances to manifest any favourable disposition towards us, even if they felt so inclined, for it was far from decided whether the French, or we, were to have the supremacy, and therefore every one who had the means betook himself elsewhere. Our position, too, in front of the town to cover the siege was anything but a comfortable one — totally unsheltered from a burning Spanish sun and unprovided with either wood or water, so that it was with no small delight that we hailed the surrender of the forts already mentioned, and the consequent retreat of the French army, for in closing up to them, it brought us to a merry country on the banks of the Douro.

Mirth and duty there, however, were, as they often are, very much at variance. Our position was a ticklish one, and required half the division to sleep in the field in front of the town each night fully accoutred, so that while we had every alternate night to rejoice in quarters, the next was one of penance in the field, which would have been tolerably fair had they been measured by the same bushel, but it could not be, for while pleasure was the order of the evening we had only to close the window-shutters to make a summer's night as long as a winter's one—but in affairs of duty, stern duty, it told in an inverse ratio ; for our vineyard beds on the alternate nights were not furnished with window-shutters, and if they had been, it would have made but little difference, for in defiance of sun, moon, or stars, we were obliged to be on our legs an hour before day-break, which in that climate and at that season, happened to be between one and two o'clock in the morning.

Our then brigadier, Sir O. Vandeleur, was rigorous on that point, and as our sleeping, bore no proportion to our waking moments, many officers would steal from the ranks to snatch a little repose under cover of the vines, and it became a highly amusing scene to see the general on horseback, threading up between the rows of bushes and ferreting out the sleepers. He netted a good number in the first cast or two, but they ultimately became too knowing for him, and had only to watch his passing up one row, to slip through the bushes into it, where they were perfectly secure for the next half hour.

I have already mentioned that Rueda was a capital wine country. Among many others there was a rough effervescent pure white wine, which I had never met with any where else, and which in warm weather was a most delicious beverage. Their wine cellars were all excavated in a sort of common, immediately outside the town; and though I am afraid to say the extent, they were of an amazing depth. It is to be presumed that the natives were all strictly honest, for we found the different cellars so indifferently provided with locks and keys, that our men, naturally inferring that good drinkers must have been the only characters in request, went to work most patriotically, without waiting to be pressed, and the cause being such a popular one, it was with no little difficulty that we kept them within bounds.

A man of ours, of the name of Taylor, wore a head so remarkably like Lord Wellington's, that he was dubbed " Sir Arthur" at the commencement of the war, and retained the name until the day of his death. At Rueda he was the servant of the good, the gallant Charley Eeles, who afterwards fell at Waterloo. Sir Arthur, in all his movements for twenty years, had been as regular as Shrewsbury clock; he cleaned his master's clothes and boots, and paraded his traps in the morning, and in the evening he got blind drunk, unless the means were wanting.

In one so noted for regularity as he was, it is but reasonable to expect that his absence at toilet time should be missed and wondered at; he could not have gone over to the enemy, for he was too true-blue for that. He could not have gone to heaven without passing through the pains of death—he was too great a sinner for that. He could not have gone downwards without passing through the aforesaid ceremony, for nobody was ever known to do so but one man, to recover his wife, and as Sir Arthur had no wife, he had surely no inducement to go there; in short the cause of his disappearance remained clouded in mystery for twenty-five hours, but would have been cleared up in a tenth part of the time, had not the rifleman, who had been in

the habit of sipping out of the same favourite
cask, been on guard in the interim, but as soon
as he was relieved, he went to pay his usual
visit, and in stooping in the dark over the edge
of the large headless butt to take his accustomed sip, his nose came in contact with that of
poor Sir Arthur, which, like that of his great
prototype, was of no mean dimensions, and who
was floating on the surface of his favourite
liquid, into which he must have dived deeper
than he intended and got swamped. Thus
perished Sir Arthur, a little beyond the prime
of life, but in what the soldiers considered, a
prime death !

Our last day at Rueda furnished an instance
so characteristic of the silence and secrecy with
which the Duke of Wellington was in the habit
of conducting his military movements, that I
cannot help quoting it.

In my former volume I mentioned that when
we were called to arms that evening, our officers
had assembled for one of their usual dances.
Our commanding officer, however, Colonel

Cameron, had been invited to dine that day with his lordship, and in addition to the staff, the party consisted of several commanding officers of regiments and others. The conversation was lively and general, and no more allusion made to probable movements than if we were likely to be fixed there for years. After having had a fair allowance of wine, Lord Wellington looked at his watch, and addressing himself to one of his staff, said, " Campbell, it is about time to be moving—order coffee." Coffee was accordingly introduced, and the guests, as usual, immediately after made their bow and retired. Our commandant in passing out of the house was rather surprised to see his lordship's baggage packed, and the mules at the door, saddled and ready to receive it, but his astonishment was still greater when he reached his own quarter, to find that his regiment was already under arms along with the rest of the troops, assembled on their alarm posts, and with baggage loaded in the act of moving off, we knew not whither!

We marched the whole of the night, and day-light next morning found us three or four leagues off, interposing ourselves between the enemy and their projected line of advance. It was the commencement of the brilliant series of movements which preceded the battle of Salamanca. Pass we on, therefore, to that celebrated field.

It was late in the afternoon before it was decided whether that day's sun was to set on a battle or our further retreat. The army all stood in position with the exception of the third division, which lay in reserve beyond the Tormes. Its commander, Sir Edward Packenham, along with the other generals of divisions, attended on the commander-in-chief, who stood on an eminence which commanded a view of the enemy's movements.

The artillery on both sides was ploughing the ground in all directions, and making fearful gaps in the ranks exposed—the French were fast closing on and around our right—the different generals had received their instructions, and waited but the final order—a few minutes must decide whether there was to be a desperate battle or a bloody retreat; when, at length,

Lord Wellington, who had been anxiously
watching their movements with his spy-glass,
called out, " Packenham, I can stand this no
longer; now is your time !" " Thank you,"
replied the gallant Packenham, " give me your
hand, my lord, and by G—d it shall be done !"
Shaking hands accordingly, he vaulted into his
saddle, and the result of his movement, as is
well known, placed two eagles, several pieces of
artillery, and four thousand prisoners in our
possession.

Packenham afterwards told a friend of mine
who was on his staff, that, while in the execution of that movement, he saw an opportunity
in which, by a slight deviation from his original
instructions, he might have cut off twenty thousand of the enemy, without greater risk to his
own division than he was about to encounter;
but he dreaded the possibility of its compro-
mising the safety of some other portion of the
army, and dared not to run the hazard.

I have, in the early part of this volume, in
speaking of individual gallantry in general,
given it as my opinion that if the merits of

every victory that had been hotly contested could be traced to the proper persons, it would be found to rest with a very few—for to those who know it not, it is inconceivable what may be effected in such situations by any individual ascending a little above mediocrity.

The day after the battle of Salamanca a brigade of heavy German dragoons, under the late Baron Bock, made one of the most brilliant charges recorded in history.

The enemy's rear guard, consisting of, I think, three regiments of infantry, flanked by cavalry and artillery, were formed in squares on an abrupt eminence, the approach to which was fetlock deep in shingle. In short, it was a sort of position in which infantry generally think they have a right to consider themselves secure from horsemen.

The Baron was at the head of two splendid regiments, and, as some of the English prints, up to that period, had been very severe upon the employment of his countrymen in the British service, he was no doubt burning with the desire

Q

for an opportunity of removing the unjust attack
that had been made upon them, and he could
not have even dreamt of one more glorious than
that alluded to.

Lord Wellington, who was up with the advanced guard, no sooner observed the dispositions of the enemy than he sent an order for the
Baron to charge them. They charged accordingly—broke through the squares, and took
the whole of the infantry—the enemy's cavalry
and artillery having fled.

Colonel May, of the British artillery, not satisfied with being the bearer of the order, gallantly
headed the charge, and fell covered with wounds,
from which he eventually recovered ; but
Lord Wellington, however much he must have
admired the action, cut him for a considerable
time in consequence, by way of marking his dis-
approval of officers thrusting themselves into
danger unnecessarily.

In an attempt so gallantly made—so glori-
ously executed—it would be invidious to exalt
one individual above another, and yet I have

every reason to believe that their success was in a great measure owing to the decisive conduct of one man.

Our battalion just rounded the hill in time to witness the end of it; and in conversing with one of the officers immediately after, he told me that their success was owing to the presence of mind of a captain commanding a squadron, who was ordered to charge the cavalry which covered a flank of the squares—that, while in full career, the enemy's horse in his front, without awaiting the shock, gave way, but, in place of pursuing them, he, with a decision calculated to turn the tide of any battle, at once brought up his outward flank, and went full tilt against a face of the square, which having until that moment been protected, was taken by surprise, and he bore down all before him!

My informant mentioned the name of the hero, but it was a severe German one, which died on the spot like an empty sound—nor have I ever since read or heard of it—so that one who ought to have filled a bright page in our history of that brilliant field, has, in all probability, passed—

> " Nor of his name or race
> Hath left a token or a trace,"

save what I have here related.

The baron, presuming that he had all the merit due to a leader on that occasion, (for I knew him only by sight,) shewed, in his own person, what we frequently see, that to be a bold man it is not necessary to be a big one. In stature he was under the middle size, slenderly made, and with a hump on one shoulder. He lived through many a bloody peninsular field to perish by shipwreck in returning to his native country.

Throughout our many hard-fought and invariably successful Peninsular fields, it used to be a subject of deep mortification for us to see the breasts of our numerous captives adorned with the different badges of the Legion of Honour, and to think that our country should never have thought their captors deserving of some little

mark of distinction, not only to commemorate
the action, but to distinguish the man who
fought, from him who did not—thereby leaving
that strongest of all corps, the *Belem Rangers*,
who had never seen a shot fired, to look as
fierce and talk as big as the best. Many officers, I see, by the periodicals, continue still to
fight for such a distinction, but the day has
gone by. No correct line could now be drawn,
and the seeing of such a medal on the breast of
a man who had no claim, would deprive it of
its chief value in the eyes of him who had.

To shew the importance attached to such dis-
tinctions in our service, I may remark that, though
the Waterloo medal is intrinsically worth two or
three shillings, and a soldier will sometimes be
tempted to part with almost any thing for drink,
yet, during the fifteen years in which I remained
with the rifles after Waterloo, I never knew a
single instance of a medal being sold, and only
one of its being pawned.

On that solitary occasion it was the property
of a handsome, wild, rattling young fellow,

named Roger Black. He, one night, at Cam-
bray, when his last copper had gone, found the
last glass of wine so good, that he could not
resist the temptation of one bottle more, for
which he left his medal in pledge with the
aubergiste, for the value of ten sous. Roger's
credit was low—a review day arrived, and he
could not raise the wind to redeem the thing he
gloried in, but, putting a bold face on it, he went
to the holder, and telling him that he had come
for the purpose of redemption, he got it in his
hands, and politely wished the landlord good
morning, telling him, as he was marching off, that
he would call and pay the franc out of the first
money he received; but the arrangement did not
suit mine host, who opposed his exit with all
the strength of his establishment, consisting of
his wife, two daughters, a well-frizzled waiter,
and a club-footed hostler. Roger, however,
painted the whole family group, ladies and all,
with a set of beautiful black eyes, and then
marched off triumphantly.

Poor Roger, for that feat, was obliged to be

paid in kind, very much against the grain of his judges, for his defence was an honest one— namely, that he had no intention of cheating the man, but he had no money, "and, by Jove, you know gentlemen, I could never think of going to a review without my medal!"

THE END.

MARCHANT, PRINTER, INGRAM-COURT, FENCHURCH-STREET.

In 8vo. price 2s.

PRUSSIA IN 1833;

ORGANIZATION OF THE ARMY OF PRUSSIA, AND HER CIVIL INSTITUTIONS.

Translated from the French of M. de Chambray. With an Appendix by General de Caraman.

" We would recommend to military readers in general, and especially to the authorities who have the destiny of the army in their hands, an attentive perusal of this work. The public will learn from it that the army of Prussia, hitherto supposed to be the worst paid force, is, in fact, better dealt with than is the case ' *with the best paid army in Europe.' "—United Service Journal.*

THE HISTORY
OF THE
KING'S GERMAN LEGION,

FROM THE PERIOD OF ITS ORGANIZATION IN 1803, TO THAT OF ITS DISSOLUTION IN 1816.
Compiled from Manuscript Documents.

By N. LUDLOW BEAMISH, Esq. F.R.S. late Major unattached.

Vol. I. 8vo. with coloured plates; price 20s. boards; to be completed in two volumes.

" Of the late war we have had histories, partial or complete, in countless abundance; but we have not seen one, displaying more moderation, more diligence in investigating the truth, or more shrewdness in deciding between conflicting statements. Though professedly merely a history of the services of the German Legion, it is, in fact, a history of the entire war; for, from ' what glorious and well-foughten field' can we record the absence of German chivalry? The work is not like others we could name—a mere compilation from newspapers and magazines. Major Beamish has left no source of information unexplored; and the access he obtained to manuscript journals has enabled him to intersperse his general narrative with interesting personal anecdotes, that render this volume as delightful for those who read for amusement, as those who read for profit."—*Athenæum.*

A TREATISE ON THE GAME OF WHIST;
BY THE LATE
ADMIRAL CHARLES BURNEY,
Author of Voyages and Discoveries in the Pacific, &c.
Second Edition. 18mo. boards, price 2s.

" The kind of play recommended in this Treatise is on the most plain, and what the Author considers the most safe principles. I have limited my endeavours to the most necessary instructions, classing them as much as the subject enabled me, under separate heads, to facilitate their being rightly comprehended and easily remembered. For the greater encouragement of the learner, I have studied brevity; but not in a degree to have prevented my endeavouring more to make the principles of the game, and the rationality of them intelligible, than to furnish a young player with a set of rules to get by rote, that he might go blindly right."

In 8vo. price 5s.

COLONIZATION;

PARTICULARLY

IN SOUTHERN AUSTRALIA:

WITH SOME REMARKS ON

SMALL FARMS AND OVER POPULATION.

By COLONEL CHARLES JAMES NAPIER, C.B.

Author of " The Colonies ; particularly the Ionian Islands."
In 1 vol. 8vo. price 9s. boards.

" I have never persuaded, or endeavoured to persuade, any one to quit England with the view of exchanging it for another country ; and I have always had great reluctance to do any thing having that tendency."—*Cobbett's Guide to Emigrants, Letter* I. *paragraph* 1.

" I have always, hitherto, advised *Englishmen* not to emigrate, even to the United States of America ; but to remain at home, *in the hope that some change* for the better would come in the course of *a few years.* It is now eleven years since I, in my YEARS' RESIDENCE, deliberately gave that advice. Not only has there, since 1818, when the YEAR'S RESIDENCE was written, been no change for the better, but things have gradually become worse and worse, in short, things have now taken that turn, and they present such a prospect for the future, that I not only think it advisable for many good people to emigrate, but I think it my duty to give them all the information I can to serve them as a guide in that very important enterprize."—*Cobbett's Guide to Emigrants, Letter* I. *paragraph* 2.

Just Published, in foolscap 8vo. price 1s.

THE NURSERY GOVERNESS.

BY ELIZABETH NAPIER;

Published after her Death by her Husband, Col. Charles James Napier, C.B.

" Hear the instructions of thy father, and forsake not the law of thy mother."—*Proverbs*, ch. i. v. 8.

" This is an admirable little book."—*True Sun.*

" The excellent instructions laid down by Mrs. Napier will, we have no doubt, prove a ' rich legacy' not only to her own children, but to those in many a nursery."—*Liverpool Chronicle.*

" Not only the nursery-governess, but the mother and daughter, especially in the higher walks of life, may read it with advantage."—*Atlas.*

" We are so convinced of its utility, that we would strongly recommend it to the diligent study of every female who has the care of a family, either as a mother or governess."—*Sun.*

Just Published, in post 8vo. price 5s.

RECOLLECTIONS AND REFLECTIONS

Relative of the Duties of Troops composing the advanced Corps of an Army.

By LIEUTENANT COLONEL I. LEACH, C.B.

Late of the Rifle Brigade.

Author of " Rough Sketches of the Life of an Old Soldier."